FIONA BARTAK
482-8669.

Sparkling Sydney

Sparkling Sydney

TEXT
BRUCE STANNARD

PHOTOGRAPHY
LEO MEIER

WELDON PUBLISHING
SYDNEY • HONG KONG • CHICAGO • LONDON

For my Father . . .

Distributed by Gary Allen Pty Ltd
9 Cooper Street, Smithfield, NSW 2164
A Kevin Weldon Production
Published by Weldon Publishing
a division of Kevin Weldon & Associates Pty Limited
372 Eastern Valley Way, Willoughby, NSW 2068, Australia
First published 1989

Editor: Robert Wilson
Designer: Maree Cunnington
Typeset in Australia by Savage Type, Brisbane
Produced in Hong Kong by Mandarin Offset

National Library of Australia Cataloguing-in-Publication entry
Stannard, Bruce.
Sparkling Sydney.
Includes index.
ISBN 0 947116 67 2.
1. Sydney (N.S.W.) — Description — 1976 — .
2. Sydney (N.S.W.) — Description — 1976 — — Views.
I. Meier, Leo, 1951 — . II. Title.
994.4'1063

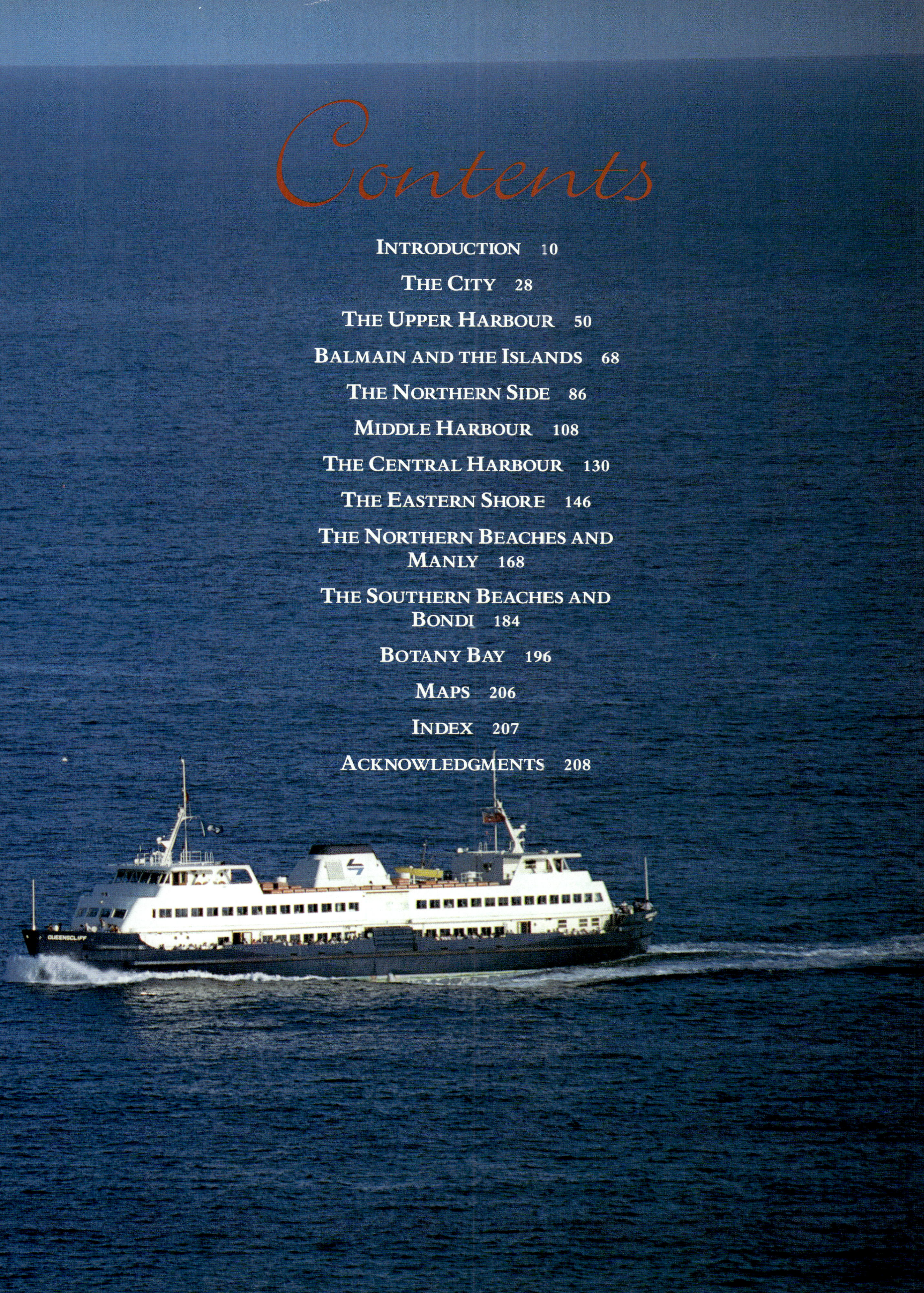

Contents

Introduction

"I know that the task would be hopeless were I to attempt to make others understand the beauty of Sydney Harbour. I can say that it is lovely but I cannot paint its loveliness. The sea runs up in various bays and coves, indenting the land all around the city so as to give a thousand different aspects to the water . . . and not of water, unbroken and unrelieved, but of water always with jutting corners of land beyond it and then again of water and then again of land. Sydney is one of the places which, when a man leaves it knowing he will never return, he cannot leave without a pang and a tear. Such is its loveliness."

ANTHONY TROLLOPE (1873)

TROLLOPE'S VIVID FIRST IMPRESSIONS, recorded well over a century ago, echo down the years to sentiments expressed in December 1916 when 21-year-old Lloyd Rees, the young artist destined to become Australia's finest painter and the man who perhaps more clearly than any other, captured the glory of the world's greatest harbour, slid in through the Heads aboard the coastal steamer, SS *Canberra*, en route from Brisbane to Melbourne.

Peering through a starboard porthole toward Manly, Rees saw what Trollope saw and miraculously, what we still see on a calm summer's morning — "the great cliffs of North Head and the harbour spread itself before me with all its bays and vistas, its sculptured foreshores and russet green vegetation and later its buildings caught in the golden light with rows and rows of them defining the contours of the hills and the whole bathed in an opalescent colour never previously seen. Is it any wonder that Sydney then and there entered my heart never to leave again?"

Rees wrote that his first glimpse was ". . . a picture in a circular frame. Opal-blue water, a band of golden sand, another of olive green trees; above them a skyline of coral pink shimmering against the limpid air. In that first long look, Sydney cast her spell and it has remained with me ever since, in spite of her brashness and disorder, the crimes she has committed against herself and above all, the opportunities she has allowed to pass — opportunities that could have made her more worthy of her setting. It was one of those calm, early mornings when all was veiled under an ethereal mist of blue through which the sun struck on golden foreshores and russet trees and depicted in creamy light the myriad facets of city buildings and the terraces defining the contours of the hills."

The novelist Trollope stayed in Sydney but briefly. Rees, who died in January 1989 at the age of 93, was to spend much of his incredibly creative life there, spellbound by the magic beauty of the harbour, splashing its loveliness onto a prodigious number of canvases. Rees called Sydney "The Source" and his "realm". "The harbour does something, its atmosphere and forms — it is a realm in which I can sink myself," he once remarked.

No two views of the harbour are ever the same, just as no two individuals will ever have exactly the same perceptions of it. For each of us, there are separate impressions, independent views that invariably add up to the same thing. Adulation.

Flying home on a sparkling morning, wheeling low over the Heads and zooming past the gleaming white shells of the Opera House to wheel left over that great grey coathanger, I sometimes think of Sydney Harbour and its surrounding roofs as a sprawling blue Gulliver beset by tiny red-hatted Lilliputians. The city skyline is immense and growing daily still taller, and yet the majesty of the waterway at its feet, stretching on and on into an infinity of sheltered coves and bays, still seems to dwarf whatever attempts mere mortals

(Previous page) After weeks of incessant rain, the summer sun bursts through heavy cloud to bathe the distant city in a dazzling light. Seen from North Head, the eerie lightshow has an almost atomic intensity.

(Right) One look at this potentially treacherous lee shore, seen from Fairfax Lookout on North Head, tells us why Cook, the great navigator, wisely opted to gain an offing once he left Botany Bay in 1770.

make to hem it in with houses and high-rise. Sydney people sometimes use a feigned indifference to mask a fierce and genuine pride in the harbour. Woe betide anyone who utters a word against it. "What do you think of the harbour?" is still the question most frequently asked by residents who already know the reply. In the '30s, a newly-arrived English visitor was so plagued by the question that he took to carrying a placard that read, not without a little sarcasm: "Yes, I've seen your 'arbour and I think it's . . . very nice."

In a world-wandering writer's life, I've been fortunate enough to have seen most of the great port cities, from Hamburg to Hong Kong, London to Liverpool, from Rio to Cape Town to Boston, Baltimore, New York, Shanghai and many more. And yet in all that time I have never seen anything to rival the splendour of Sydney Harbour.

Sydney's importance as Australia's prime commercial port may be somewhat eclipsed these days with the development of the container terminal at Port Botany, and yet it remains, above all else, a place of sublime natural beauty, with the foreshore of distinctive biscuit-coloured sandstone topped by towering, pale pink angophoras which grow, as they always have, right at the saltwater's edge. Yet despite two centuries of European habitation, there is so much which remains not only in pristine condition but miraculously free and open to anyone who cares to enjoy it.

I take considerable pride in the fact that, like four generations of my family, I was born on and raised by the harbour. Since 1850 when William Stannard established himself as one of the infant colony's first licensed watermen, plying his 18ft cedar skiff for hire from a little stone cottage at Man O' War Steps, near where the Opera House now stands, the name Stannard has become synonymous with the harbour and its watercraft. For almost 140 years, Stannard's ferries, launches, lighters and tugboats have been an integral part of harbour life. And that's still the case.

That intimate family connection with the harbour has been doubly important to me. I grew up on what was then the dark side of the Bridge, the Balmain waterfront, hard by the lee of Goat Island. As a kid I played Huck Finn on home-made rafts rigged with sails cut from my mother's cotton sheets. I paddled tin canoes fashioned from roofing iron, tomato crates and gooey tar scooped from blistered roads on broiling summer days. At night, I could hear the rhythmic slap, slap, slap of waves washing on sandstone walls, and yes, even the chattering of water rats. I liked nothing better than to lie in bed, watching the navigation lights on the last of the ferries as they projected weird shapes that crept in through the windows and slid like ghostly apparitions around the walls and out again.

My father knew every part of the harbour, and it seemed everyone on it knew him. With the exception of the war years, when he commanded RAAF air-sea rescue boats in the Pacific, he spent his life driving launches and lighters and tugs on the harbour, and through his eyes I came to see and appreciate its light and its shade. I went with him everywhere and he allowed me to see it in good times and in bad, in fair weather and foul. I've seen the water black with oil and oozing muck. I've seen it sparkle on a bright winter morning like a million diamonds scattered on a bright blue baize. I've seen a black nor'easter rip a racing fleet to shreds and I've felt that strange excitement underlayed with fear when the salt wind bites, and the air is white with spume in a shrieking southerly buster.

For almost half a century, scarcely a day has passed without I've given thanks for a life on the waterfront. And I make no apologies for what is an unashamedly emotional connection. It may well be the Irish in me (my great-grandfather on my mother's side was an O'Brien from County Donegal), but with a harbour-family connection stretching back over near 140 years, I don't mind admitting to a deep sense of spiritual kinship with that magic blend of sunshine, sandstone and salt water that is uniquely Sydney. Sydney Harbour has been mother and father to me — a source of inspiration and instruction, of wonder and of joy.

(Above) Tiny Washaway Beach at the base of Grotto Point is aptly named. Overlooking The Sound, the beach lies exposed to the fierce southerlies that often send enormous seas pounding into the beach.

(Pages 14–15) Sunset casts a golden glow over the main harbour as a surfboat crew sets out on an evening training run.

Like many Australians, I regard the harbour as the closest thing we have to a sacred national site. Like a brilliant gem with a thousand facets, the harbour cannot be properly appreciated until each of those facets — the bays and coves and inlets, the rivers and beaches, the reefs and the islands have been explored and explained. It should be a very personal experience. This book is not designed to replace that personal experience but to enhance it with sympathetic words, and images of outstanding quality by one of the world's most distinguished nature photographers, Leo Meier. Meier's magnificent photographs present the most complete and the most compelling pictorial record of the harbour ever made.

It has always seemed to me a great pity that the honour of uncovering the pristine glory of Sydney Harbour did not fall to my great hero, Captain James Cook. The greatest navigator of his age, and the man whose meticulous charts did so much to clear the way for Australia's eventual European settlement, Cook saw the harbour's two kilometre-wide mouth and named it Port Jackson, after his zealous friend and early patron, Sir George Jackson, Judge-Advocate of the Royal Navy's Home Fleet and a Joint Secretary of the British Admiralty. But for reasons that, more than two centuries later, still remain the subject of speculation and debate, Cook decided not to come about and enter. And yet to anyone who has sailed that coast, Cook's probable reasons should be clear enough.

After all, he had lain at anchor three leagues — or 12 kilometres — to the south in Botany Bay for the best part of a week, re-watering and replenishing fuel supplies. Also during that time the botanist, Joseph (later Sir Joseph) Banks, and his assistants had gathered a veritable cornucopia of exotic plant specimens that all but filled the great cabin on the little bark, *Endeavour*. Cook ordered the anchors weighed at daylight on Sunday, May 6 1770, set sail in a light nor'west breeze and headed out of the Bay's uncomfortably shallow and exposed anchorage, slowly heading nor'nor'east, along that vast, unknown and potentially fatal shore. By mid-morning, the breeze went round to the south "as if a benediction were being laid upon me". By noon, Cook's observations in latitude 30° 50′ south placed *Endeavour* "about 2 or 3 miles from the land and abreast of a Bay or Harbour wherein there appeared to be safe anchorage".

That, as it turned out, was the understatement of his life. But at that distance, Cook had no way of knowing he was peering at the entrance to the finest harbour in the world. Squinting through his glass from the heaving quarterdeck of the *Endeavour*, what he saw in the distance was the great bulk of North Head, the crumbled cliffs of South Head and between them the confusing loom of Middle Head. The three massive headlands, seen together like that, often perform a confusing visual trick. To anyone unfamiliar with the landforms, what one sees from that range might easily be mistaken for little more than an indentation. Sailing up the coast, it's not until South Head is almost abeam that that incredible body of water begins to properly reveal itself, stretching as far as the eye can see to the west as the Main Harbour, to the north toward Manly as North Harbour and still further around Middle Head and into the delightful shelter of Middle Harbour. Bare statistics alone cannot convey the magnitude of the place but for the record, the harbour's total area of sheltered deep water is said to be about 55 square kilometres while the shoreline stretches over an incredible 250 kilometres.

The thrill of being the first Europeans to uncover properly the harbour had to wait a further 18 years, until Australia's first colonial governor, Captain Arthur Phillip, and the men who accompanied him in three small boats, rowed and sailed north from Botany Bay in search of a better anchorage for the 11 ships of the First Fleet. At Botany Bay, the lack of good fresh water, the poor quality of the soil and the exposed nature of their anchorage had led Phillip to seek an alternative almost as soon as he arrived.

(Right) Joggers puff past an ancient Port Jackson fig at Lady Macquarie's Chair, the eastern arm of Farm Cove where from 1810 to 1815, Elizabeth, the wife of Governor Lachlan Macquarie, took her ease in the Government Domain.

The Pacific does not always match its name. Aeons of pounding have reduced the base of Bondi's cliffs to broad rock ledges etched with cracks through which the waves race then beat a frothy retreat.

(Overleaf) While a summer rainstorm drapes the city in a veil of grey, the harbour, from Rose Bay to Clarke Island, shimmers beneath a silver sun.

Early on the "mild and serene" morning of January 22 1788, Phillip took the ships' boats, and in company with Captain John Hunter, commander of the fleet's armed tender, HMS *Sirius*, the Judge-Advocate, Captain David Collins, the Master of the brig HMS *Supply*, David Blackburn, and the Master of the *Sirius*, James Keltie, together with a party of Marines for their protection, set out on a northbound course through the gentle swells at Botany's heads and up the coast. Hunter's journal says they were "intending if we could, to reach what Captain Cook has called Broken Bay". Phillip's own version says it was "resolved therefore to examine Port Jackson, a bay mentioned by Captain Cook as immediately to the north of this". Collins claims they intended to examine both places.

It really doesn't matter where they were going. The point is, they got there. And what a sublime moment that must have been. No matter how many times I sail in through Sydney Heads, my mind invariably goes racing back over the centuries in an imaginary replay of that moment when Phillip and his men swung west around South Head's low, shelving sandstone face and found themselves in a paradise of calm and incredibly crystal-clear indigo water. According to Hunter, "it had rather unpromising appearance, on entering between the outer heads or capes that form its entrance, which are high, rugged and perpendicular cliffs; but we had not gone far in, before we discovered a large branch extending to the southward; into this we went and soon found ourselves perfectly land-locked with a good depth of water".

Phillip was somewhat less constrained. In a letter to Lord Sydney, the Home Secretary, who was responsible for colonial affairs, he penned his most quoted lines . . . "We had the satisfaction to find, one of the finest harbours in the world. One in which a thousand sail of the line might ride in perfect security."

John White, the Surgeon-General to the fleet, wrote his own impressions, which were to be published in London two years later: "Port Jackson, I believe to be, without exception, the finest and most extensive harbour in the Universe and at the same time the most secure, being safe from all the winds that blow."

Capt.-Lieut. Watkin Tench, who was in charge of the Marine detachment on the *Charlotte* and official scribe, in his *Narrative of the Expedition to Botany Bay*, described the harbour as "a port superior, in extent and excellency, to all we had seen before".

There have been many factual and some fanciful descriptions of what the harbour was like in January 1788 but none more vivid nor compelling than the word picture painted by the distinguished art critic and historian Robert Hughes. In his book, *The Fatal Shore*, Hughes likens the moment to the breaking open of a time capsule. "The Aborigines and the fauna around them had possessed the landscape since time immemorial, and no human eye had seen them," he wrote. "Now the protective glass of distance broke, in an instant, never to be restored. To imagine the place one should begin at North Head, the upper mandible of the harbour. Here, Australia stops; its plates of sandstone breaking off like biscuits whose crumbs, the size of cottages, lie jumbled 250 feet below, at the surging ultramarine rim of the Pacific. A ragged wall of creamy-brown sandstone, fretted by the incessant wind, runs north to a glazed horizon. To the east, the Pacific begins its 7000-mile arc toward South America. Long swells grind into the cliff in a boiling white lather, flinging veils of water a hundred feet into the air. At the meetings of its ancient planes of rock, sea and sky — mass, energy and light — one can grasp why the Aborigines called North Head *Boree*, 'the enduring one'. The sandstone is the bone and root of the coast. On top of the cliff, the soil is thin and the scrub sparse. There are banksia bushes with their sawtooth-edge leaves and dried seed-cones like multiple, jabbering mouths. Against this austere grey-green, the occasional red or blue scribble of a flower looks startling. But further back to the west, the sandstone ledges dip down into the harbour, separating it into scores

of inlets. In 1788 these sheltered coves were densely wooded. The largest trees were eucalypts: red gums, angophoras, scribbly gums and a dozen others. Until the late eighteenth century no European had ever seen a eucalypt and very strange they must have looked, with their strings of hanging, half-shed bark, their smooth wrinkling joints (like armpits, elbows or crotches), their fluent gesticulations and haze of perennial foliage. Not evergreens but evergreys: the soft spatially deceitful background colour of the Australian bush, monotonous-looking at first sight but rippling with nuances to the acclimatised eye.

"In the gullies, where streams of water slid from pool to pool leaving beards of rusty algae on their sandstone lips, giant cabbage tree palms grew, their damp shade supporting a host of ferns and mosses. Yellow sprays of mimosa flashed in the sun along the ridges and there were stands of blackboy trees, their dry spear of a stalk shooting up from a drooping hackle of fronds. Most of the ground was sandy and thin but parts of the harbour foreshores held, to the relief of Captain John Hunter, Phillip's second-in-command, . . . 'tolerable land . . . which may be cultivated without waiting for its being cleared of wood . . .'."

Phillip and his men landed first at a delightful little sandy beach in the lee of South Head to which they gave the name Camp Cove. They slept there under Marine guard, on the beach beside their boats.The following day they split up and rowed off to begin the harbour's exploration. What Phillip sought was a place where the 11 ships of his First Fleet could anchor close by the shore and easily discharge their 1400-odd people and their stores. Although there is still some dispute over the actual number of convicts there are believed to have been a total of 759 convicts plus 16 or 18 children. The combined crews of the ships totalled 443 and the Marine guard, 212.

After the disappointments at not finding Cook's promised land at Botany Bay, Phillip was anxious to uncover the best possible source of clean, fresh water and land that could be easily cleared for cultivation. The place he found and subsequently named Sydney Cove after Lord Sydney must surely have exceeded any of his expectations.

According to Captain Tench, Phillip's boat left Camp Cove and moved up the harbour about four miles to the westward, "till we arrived at a small snug cove on the southern side on whose banks the plan of our operations was destined to commence". According to Phillip's account, preference was given to the cove "which had the finest spring of water and in which ships can anchor so close to the shore that at a very small expense quays may be constructed at which the largest vessels may unload". Sydney Cove was then said to have been "about half a mile in length."

On January 23 Phillip and his boat party returned to the fleet at anchor in Botany Bay and issued the orders for the move, which was to take place at dawn on January 26. In Phillip's absence, two French ships, *L'Astrolabe* and *La Boussole*, were seen off the coast attempting, unsuccessfully because of the offshore breeze, to gain entry to the bay. The ships, under the command of the Comte de La Perouse, tried to get into the bay for two days before the wind became an onshore sea breeze. At dawn on the 26th, Hunter sent a boat out to show the French the channel. On board the *L'Astrolabe*, the English officers found La Perouse with a copy of Captain Cook's chart — the same chart that had brought the British fleet safely to the far side of the earth — spread out on his binnacle. La Perouse had unstinting praise for the English navigator and not least for the accuracy of his charts.

Although the British and the French were then at peace, Phillip was naturally anxious to establish and reinforce King George III's claim to Port Jackson. On January 23, Phillip left aboard the armed tender *Supply* and sailed north to prepare for the arrival of the fleet. The English ships scrambled out of the bay — some of them nearly colliding in their haste — almost as soon as the Frenchmen came to anchor. At dusk the transports and store ships were all at anchor within Sydney Cove while the armed tender *Sirius* stood guard.

Summer twilight over Sydney. The old sailor's adage, Red Sky at Night, Sailor's Delight, promises a fine, clear, warm day ahead. This view, westward from North Head, overlooks the harbour's mouth known as The Sound.

What better way to begin the day than with cafe au lait beneath the parasols of the Opera House's Western Broadwalk? Across the semi-Circular Quay is berthed the Sitmar Line's cruise ship, *Fairstar*.

When the first of the Marines and male convicts landed on the western side of the cove they stepped ashore into thick woods and made their way around to the head of the cove where the cool freshwater stream drained from the marshlands later reclaimed for what is now Hyde Park. There, the Union Jack is said to have been hoisted from the branches of an enormous casuarina tree. The female convicts — the youngest 13 and the oldest 82 — were obliged to stay on the ships for a further three days until the heavy work of clearing the ground and preparing the encampment was complete.

In her excellent *Companion Guide to Sydney*, novelist Ruth Park paints a compelling picture of the sights and sounds and smells that must have overwhelmed many of the convicts. ''What the female convicts saw from the ships' rails were low hills, tawny blonde with summer that rolled on to finish in hyacinth heat haze'', she wrote. ''This monotonous hillscape had a strange effect on the Europeans. It inspired melancholy sensations reminding one of a tempestuous sea transfixed into leaden stillness. To the east lay a long spit like the neck of a swan outstretched on the water. It was almost entirely composed of oyster, mussel and scallop shells, a 30-foot depth of bleached white shells left behind after thousands of years of Aboriginal picnics on this bountiful shore.''

The spit was named Cattle Point because it was here that the first stock were landed. For 50 years it provided the little encampment at Sydney Cove with the raw material for burning the lime which was then essential to bind mud and clay into a tolerable building mortar. Cattle Point later became Bennelong Point, the pre-eminent site chosen in the 1960s as the home of the spectacular Sydney Opera House.

Ruth Park climbed into a novelist's time machine, transporting herself back through the centuries to record one of the most eloquent descriptions of Sydney Cove as it must have been: ''To the right were the long sandstone ledges and lintels of what was to be Dawes Point, dipping down into fine, deep water, the horny lizard spine of the ridge scantily clad with rufous fuzz, as though some prehistoric bushfire had flashed down the promontory and left it bare of all but wildflowers, grass trees and sea-stained scrub.''

No one now knows what the Aboriginals named the beautiful year-round ''run of clear water'' which had made Phillip choose Sydney Cove for a settlement. Phillip, who later had convicts cut deep sandstone tanks in its bed, simply called it the Tank Stream.

According to Ruth Park, ''all round the rivulet stood a majestic forest of Sydney red gums, huge myrtles with flesh of luminous rosiness. There were mimosas (speedily renamed 'wattle' because these small flowering trees were the first to be cut down and used in wattle and daub huts) and there were also turpentines, ironbark, blackbutt and the strange grass tree or blackboy, lifting its lance rimmed with downy light. In the humid recesses of the gullies grew orchids, mosses, ferns and a battalion of immensely tall cabbage tree palms which were cut down quick smart (for thatching) so that within a year not a palm remained. With equal celerity the settlers were to destroy the Tank Stream itself. Having no knowledge of semi-tropical water systems in spongy topsoil and decayed vegetation, they stripped the land bare, hoed up the shallow earth and in no time lost that as well by erosion.

''But on that first January 26th, all was calm, fertile and being January, alive with bird and insect life. Christmas beetles still flipped like tossed sovereigns into the apple gums and the whole vale vibrated with giant cicadas playing their steely castanets till the ears rang. Flocks of waterhen scurried off to the upper reaches of the Tank Stream. Ducks left hurriedly for the tranquil Botany Swamps. The new species had arrived and the old ones, which had been safe against the black people's scanty requirements, began to die.

''Only the sandstone bones of the land remain. The hills have become slighter in grade, the gullies filled, the sea driven back, a forest of steel and concrete cacti has sprung up from the rind of the earth.''

ROYALE
ROYALE
SYDNEY
ROYALE

The City

"Oh, there never dawned a morning, in the long and lonely days,
But I thought I saw the ferries streaming out across the bays —
And as fresh and fair in fancy did the picture rise again
As the sunrise flushed the city from Woollahra to Balmain;

With the sunny water frothing round the liners black and red,
And the coastal schooners working by the loom of Bradley's Head,
With the whistles and the sirens that re-echo far and wide —
All the life and light and beauty that belong to Sydney-side.

And the dreary cloud-line never veiled the end of one day more,
But the city set in jewels rose before me from 'The Shore'.
Round the sea-world shine the beacons of a thousand ports o' call,
But the harbour-lights of Sydney are the grandest of them all."

Sydney-side. HENRY LAWSON (1898)

LAWSON, THE MASTER OF the Australian bush ballad, also had a poet's eye for the beauty of Sydney Harbour. Often when I cross that great coathanger of a bridge, southbound on a clear, black night with all those white lights blazing in the city and the great arching shells of the Opera House glistening down there in the gloom like some fantastic creamy crustacean, I find myself reciting his lines, thinking of the moustachioed poet in the droopy hat and wondering, would Lawson recognise his beloved Sydney-side now? Would he still feel the same affinity with the water or would he, in the end, prefer the bush?

So much of the harbour has changed in the century since he wrote those lines and yet, miraculously, so much remains the same. The City of Sydney, and Circular Quay in particular, often seem to be in a more or less constant state of being torn down and thrown up. Lawson, I suspect, might shake his head at the relentless pace of it all.

Sydney sometimes seems obsessed with change almost for the sake of change. When I was a child aboard my father's boats, I used to cringe as we chugged under the Bridge's towering arch, ploughing a white foamy furrow through the cool green gloom of its shadow before we wheeled hard to starboard heading into the Quay. There, all was change. As the first of the waterfront skyscrapers, the AMP tower on the corner of Alfred and Phillip Streets, rose up in its giant steel skeleton, people stood gaping in awe at what was then the biggest building in Australia.

Quickly it was joined by Goldfields House at the other end of Alfred Street and then by dozens of others, marching uptown, each trying to outdo the other in a brazen show of concrete and glass. More than any other Australian city, Sydney has been characterised by a relentless, restless energy. Apart from the magnificence of Macquarie Street's historic precinct, which runs from Hyde Park to the Opera House, The Rocks, where a clutch of historic buildings and Victorian terraces cling defiantly to the Quay's western shore, and one or two other isolated places, Sydney, the city by the sea, seems to be forever pummelled by incessant waves of constant construction and demolition.

One of the loudest laments, at least from those of us who grew up on and around the Quay, is heard for the disappearance of so many of the marvellous old waterfront pubs whose patrons, a broad cross-section of salty humanity, ebbed and flowed like the harbour tides. Up at the far eastern end of Alfred Street was the tiny First and Last, a six o'clock opener and a favourite haunt of wharfies and journalists. One of the oldest of the waterfront

(Right) Cheek by granite jowl in the city's central business district, office towers and apartment blocks are bathed in the ethereal glow of a summer sunset.

(Previous page) *Royale*, one of Charlie Rosman's fleet of passenger ferries (the others are the *Radar* and the *Regalia*) bustles toward Circular Quay with city-bound commuters, all of whom swear there is no finer way to get to work.

In the blue way above the gleaming Opera House shells, wispy cirrus cloud leaves telltale feathers that point to high altitude wind. Historic Sydney Cove lies in a green calm on this glorious summer morning.

(Right) Sydney Harbour continues to yield a rich harvest of seafood. The traditional Italian fishing families have moved up the social ladder and are handing over their nets and their boats to Vietnamese fishermen.

pubs, it also was one of the most colourful with its own cast of characters that often seemed to have materialised straight out of the pages of Richard Henry Dana's classic tale of the sea, *Two Years Before The Mast.* There were chantymen and poets, seamen who played clackety tunes on bones and spoons and combs, a chap with a wheezy harmonium and another with a screechy fiddle. The beer was cold and the air invariably blue with a cigarette fug and the oaths of hard men and even harder women. It was a throwback to a rollicking past that we are not likely to see again.

The First and Last is gone now, replaced by a glass and concrete tower block featuring the kind of super-luxury apartments only multimillionaires can afford. At the famous Ship Inn, up the road on the corner of Pitt and Alfred Streets, the pub walls were covered with a wonderful array of old shipping photographs and nautical memorabilia tacked up by the seamen and wharfies, the customs men and shipping clerks, the launch drivers, tugboat hands and the water police who in the late afternoon, all stood shoulder to shoulder, boozing in the broad front bar.

In the late 19th century, in the twilight of the great age of sail, one of those who braced the bar and reflected on the Sydney atmosphere of those times was Joseph Conrad, the great writer who immortalised the glory of sail in so many of his brilliant novels and short stories. In *The Mirror of the Sea*, a collection of the best of Conrad's shorter works on shipboard life, he writes with particular affection of Circular Quay.

"These towns of the Antipodes, not so great then as they are now," he says, "took an interest in the shipping, the running links with 'home', whose numbers confirmed the sense of their growing importance. They made it part and parcel of their daily interests. This was especially the case in Sydney where from the heart of the fair city, down the vista of important streets, could be seen the wool clippers lying at the Circular Quay — no walled prison-house of a dock that, but the integral part of one of the finest, most beautiful, vast and safe bays the sun has ever shone upon. Now, numbers of great steam liners lie at these berths, always reserved for the sea aristocracy — grand and imposing enough ships, but here today and gone next week; whereas the general cargo, emigrant and passenger clippers of my time, rigged with heavy spars and built on fine lines, used to remain for months together waiting for their load of wool. Their names attained the dignity of household words.

"On Sundays and holidays the citizens trooped down, on visiting bent and the lonely officer on duty solaced himself by playing the cicerone — especially to the citizenesses with engaging manners and a well-developed sense of the fun that may be got out of the inspection of a ship's cabins

Meticulous attention to detail gives these restored town houses in The Rocks an authentic Victorian air. A rich architectural vein has led to the entire area being jealously guarded by heritage legislation.

(Previous page) Intense summer heat in Sydney often brings with it soaring humidity, violent electrical storms and torrential rain. But invariably the city gains relief from cool ''southerly busters''. After the change, a rainbow arcs up from Bennelong Point.

and state-rooms. The tinkle of more or less untuned cottage pianos floated out of the open stern-ports till the gas lamps began to twinkle in the streets and the ship's night-watchman, coming sleepily on-duty after his unsatisfactory day slumbers, hauled down the flags and fastened a lighted lantern at the break of the gangway. The night closed rapidly upon the silent ships with their crews on shore. Up a short, steep ascent by the King's Head pub, patronised by the cooks and stewards of the fleet, the voice of a man crying 'Hot Saveloys!' at the end of George Street where the cheap eating houses (sixpence a meal) were kept by Chinamen, is heard at regular intervals.''

The old wooden wharves along the eastern side of the Quay where Conrad's clippers waited for wool have long since been torn down to expand the space for ferries and to make room for a broad and beautifully paved and sheltered public promenade leading out to the Opera House at the very tip of Bennelong Point. In my mind's eye, I see the towering clippers even now, the *Cutty Sark*, the *Tweed*, the *Macquarie* and the *Invercargill*, lined up, patiently waiting for the bullock drays to lumber down from the bush.

The head of the Quay and its entire western face also were given a wash and brush-up for the bicentennial celebrations. Paving, landscaping and the meticulous restoration of John Cadman's Cottage, the delightful little stone house of the colonial waterman not far from the overseas shipping terminal, have at last linked the historic waterfront with The Rocks, that marvellous jumble of terraces and cottages, tiny shops and pubs whose simple 19th century elegance provides us all with a vivid reminder of the way the entire Circular Quay precinct must have looked in the halcyon days when sailing ships moored so close that their thrusting jib-booms and figureheads reached right over the roadway.

Sydney's central business district may look big from the water's edge but compared with sprawling Melbourne, it is in fact relatively small. Contained as it is by the broad green buffer of the Royal Botanic Gardens to the east, Darling Harbour to the west and Circular Quay to the North, the city has been forced to go higher and higher until today, for better or for worse, it boasts a spectacular skyline not too dissimilar to Manhattan. The pressure is such that the city is now marching southward and to the north, leaping over the harbour to North Sydney where, in the manner of Buda and Pest, Hungary's twin cities split by the Danube, twin Sydneys are rising on facing shores.

When the British military engineer, Sir George Gipps, took over as Governor of New South Wales in 1838, he enlisted the help of a brother officer from the Royal Engineers, Captain George Barney, in reshaping Sydney Cove into the famous horseshoe-shaped Semi-Circular Quay. The system of convict transportation, the backbone of the colony's early growth, ended in 1841, and the construction of what has become known as Circular Quay was the last major engineering project undertaken with convict labour. The project involved the reclamation of four hectares of mudflats behind a huge sandstone seawall, with thousands of convict labourers gouging and transporting stone fill from Cockatoo Island and Rock Island (Fort Denison), the Argyle Cut in The Rocks and the Tarpeian Rock on the cove's eastern shore.

The Harbour Bridge leaps from Dawes Point to Milson's Point. The terraces and historic Garrison Church are all protected under heritage legislation.

During the early years of the 20th century, the area at the head of the Quay was given over to wharves for the dozens of picturesque paddlewheeler ferries that

Like the bridge of some futuristic aircraft carrier, the bold revamped facade of the International Terminal dominates the western side of Sydney Cove. (Right) Doyles at Circular Quay, opposite the Opera House and directly below the International Terminal on the western side of Sydney Cove, must surely be one of the best-positioned seafood restaurants in the world.

daily brought thousands of commuters to the city from the suburbs springing up around the harbour's foreshores. Ferries are to Sydney what gondolas are to Venice. And although the colours of their livery and indeed their size, shape and power have changed drastically over the years, the ferries still provide the best and least expensive method of harbour travel. From Circular Quay, ferries stream out to many parts of the harbour. The first ferry, the Rose Hill Packet, was launched from the yard of convict shipwright James Underwood on the western side of the mouth of the Tank Stream in 1789. The first substantial vessel built in Australia, she was a 10-ton hoy, a vessel both sailed and rowed, which was designed to take passengers and stores from Sydney Cove, 20 kilometres up the Parramatta River to the settlement at Rose Hill.

As the population grew, so too did the demand for harbour transportation. Throughout the 19th century the demand was such that scores of watermen were able to continue the tradition born on the River Thames, rowing their long, narrow-gutted pulling boats to all points of the harbour. One of the Stannard family's most treasured possessions is the faded parchment Waterman's Licence issued to William Stannard in 1858. The licence sets out a schedule of fares and rates. One could be rowed from ''any of the Circular Quay stairs'' to Bradley's Head, Cremorne, and anywhere in between for two shillings. The 12-kilometre row from Circular Quay to Manly cost 10 shillings while the haul to Darling Harbour and Balmain was two shillings.

When the watermen were not busy rowing passengers back and forth, they contracted with the government to haul stone from the quarries on Goat Island and Neutral Bay either to the Quay or to Fort Denison.

Fort Denison is one of the most interesting of all the harbour's islands. Lying off the mouth of Sydney Cove and close by the entrance to Woolloomooloo Bay, it occupied a unique strategic position which was to guarantee its survival, not so much as an island but as a heavily fortified citadel. Known to the Aboriginal people as ''Mattewai'', meaning small, rocky island, it was recorded by Captain Phillip when he and his boat's crew became the first Europeans to row up the harbour in January 1788. Although the barren sandstone outcrop which rose sharply from the water to form a 25-metre pyramid was known simply as Rock Island, it is believed that Captain John Hunter, Master of the *Sirius*, who was responsible for the first survey of the harbour, gave it its enduring colloquial name of Pinchgut. Although there is still some debate as to whether the term originally was a reference to the bread and water conditions under which convicts were sometimes kept there, it is now generally accepted that the name derives from 18th century naval parlance. Pinchgut simply referred to a point where the navigable channel was extremely narrow.

At Australia's first criminal court hearing, held in Sydney on February 8 1788, Thomas Hill, a convict found guilty of stealing biscuits from another convict was, as

AMP

ESSO

Surgeon John White noted in his diary, "ordered to a barren rock, or little island, in the middle of the harbour, there to remain on bread and water for a stated time". The "bread" was ship's biscuits known as hard tack, while the water came from barrels aboard the *Sirius* anchored off the mouth of Sydney Cove. Hill was there for a week. During the first few months of the settlement, while the colony was finding its feet and a stockade was being built, other convicts were sent to the island as punishment for stealing food, so that the old naval term, pinchgut, became doubly appropriate.

The island is said to have been a fishing spot favoured by Aboriginals who paddled canoes which, according to Watkin Tench, were "nothing more than a large piece of bark tied up at both ends with vines". The Aboriginals abandoned the island, never to return, when in 1798 Governor Hunter decided to make an example of a murderer named Morgan. Hunter had the man strung up on a gibbet on the island and there the remains swung for three years. The macabre sight is recorded in the journal of "General" Joseph Holt, transported for his part in the Irish Rebellion of 1798. Holt sailed into Port Jackson aboard the brig *Minerva*, a convict transport bringing "rebel felons" from Ireland in January 1800.

"Just at day light we entered Sidney Heads we then fird a Gun for a pilot but none Appeard", Holt wrote. "Mr Harrison brot forward the map gave Order, as it Directed him we saild up by pinch Gut island, the fist thing I observed was the skeleton of a man in gibbets by Name of Morgan, whose Crime I Discoverd to be wilful Murder. We pafsd by Garden Islnd and Came into Sidney Cove Cast Anchor at 11 o'clock 11th Jan., 1800."

Apart from Captain George Barney's monumental work in engineering the construction of Circular Quay, his other enduring monument is Fort Denison and its magnificent martello tower. Although the tower and its fortifications are popularly believed to owe their origins to the paranoia that surrounded the long drawn out and bloody British and Russian conflict in the Crimea, the initial impetus for Barney's work came in the unlikely form of a squadron of friendly American men-o'-war which, under the command of Commodore Charles Wilkes, sailed unchallenged and under cover of darkness, right up the harbour to anchor off Sydney Cove on Saturday, November 30 1839. The American sloops *Vincennes* (780 tons) and *Peacock* (580 tons) and five lesser warships which were on an "exploratory trip to the South Seas", arrived off the Heads at 8pm. With a fair wind but no pilot, Wilkes decided, as he wrote, to "run up and anchor off the Cove". "At half past ten we quietly dropped anchor off the Cove in the midst of the shipping without anyone having the least idea of our arrival. When the good people of Sydney looked abroad in the morning they were much astonished to see two men-o'-war lying among their shipping . . . A few days before our arrival it had been debated in [the Legislative] Council whether more effective means of fortification were not necessary for the harbour. The idea of this being wanted was ridiculed by the majority, but the entrance of our ships by night seems to have changed their

Fort Denison's martello tower has stood guard at the entrance to Circular Quay since the days of the Crimean War, when a Russian counter-offensive through Sydney Cove was thought possible.
(Left) Moonrise over the Opera House. On a soft, warm summer's evening such as this, what prima donna could quibble with so magnificent a setting?
(Previous page) Southbound, northbound, commuters dash across the southern approach to the Harbour Bridge in the lull before the early morning peak hour.

opinion. Had war existed, we might, after firing the shipping and reducing the great part of the town to ashes, have effected a retreat before daybreak, in perfect safety."

Work began immediately on an ambitious £5000 plan to fortify Pinchgut, Kirribilli and Bradley's Head. The scheme, put forward by Captain Barney, involved the enormous task of completely levelling the rocky pinnacle on Pinchgut and replacing it with a fortress fashioned from some 8000 tonnes of stone cut and beautifully dressed in enormous honey-coloured blocks. When work started in 1841, the colony's fiery Scottish preacher, the Reverend John Dunmore Lang, condemned the island's destruction as an act of "downright vandalism" akin to the "Communists of Paris pulling down the famous triumphal column in the Place Vendome". But work on the fort had scarcely begun when the authorities in London decided against the expenditure of such vast sums on faraway citadels. Work was brought to a halt until 1855 when word of the conflict in the Crimea peninsula finally reached the colony, which was then under the governorship of Sir William Denison. Under Barney's guidance, the walls of the fort were made almost four metres thick at the base and about three metres at the top.

Manned by Royal Artillerymen, the fort's armament consisted of two 10-inch guns and 10 eight-inch 32 pounders. Fortunately the guns never fired a shot in anger. Three of the 32-pounders were hoisted into position in the tower before its completion in 1857. Getting them out today would involve dismantling the tower itself. The tower also houses the light, originally oil-fired, which was first lit in 1858. Up there also on public display is the great polished brass gong that sounded its warning to 19th century mariners whenever the harbour was shrouded in heavy fog. The light and the fog alarm are now much less romantically powered by electricity.

Contrary to popular belief, convicts were never housed on Fort Denison. There are three triangular cells at the base of the tower but these were never intended to be used other than as a place of safe storage for gunpowder and shot.

Since no fort is complete without its own independent water supply, a well was hewn out of the solid rock, eight metres long, four metres wide and four metres deep with a capacity of more than 100 000 litres. Although water is now piped across to the fort from Garden Island, the well is kept topped up by rainfall and remains in excellent condition. The Maritime Services Board is responsible for the fort's maintenance and a Board employee and his family live there permanently, sole occupants of one of the most exclusive pieces of real estate in Australia.

It was George Barney who in 1857 initiated the change of name from Pinchgut to Fort Denison in the Governor's honour. Denison's personal correspondence makes it clear that so far as he was concerned, the fort owed its existence not so much to the so-called Russian menace as it did to the concern of the colonial authorities that a "Yankee filibustering expedition" might launch an armed assault on Sydney's gold vaults which were bulging with gold awaiting shipment to England. The rumour had no foundation. Nevertheless, at the outbreak of the American Civil War in 1861 when it was feared the Union states might declare war on Britain and her colonies, a battery of three 68-pounders and 10 eight-inch guns was mounted near the present Hornby Light on Inner South Head about 30 metres above the highwater mark. Denison's concern for American intentions highlights the extraordinary irony in the fact that almost a century later the fort was struck by a shell from the American battleship, USS *Chicago*, firing wildly at night in response to the attack by Japanese midget submarines.

Four of the 24-metre submarines are believed to have been launched from a mother-ship off the Heads shortly after nightfall on May 31 1942. One was almost immediately detected and sunk. The crew of another, caught in the boom and net defences, chose to

Ferries in one form or another have been plying in and out of Circular Quay since early settlement. These vessels, sturdy, steel double-enders, are decked out in the cream and blue of the State Transit Authority.

Like a brightly burnished table, the watery expanse of Walsh Bay offers up shimmering reflections from city towers, topped this evening by rainclouds.

Criss-crossing the harbour in a never-ending routine, the harbour's working vessels, ferries, fishing trawlers, cruise boats and ships ply the busiest stretch just north and east of Sydney Cove.

blow themselves up, while two others were able to penetrate the defences and target the massive allied fleet which lay at anchor around the naval base at Garden Island. One was detected and destroyed by depth charges before it could fire its torpedoes. The other, which surfaced and was engaged by Australian and American warships, fired two torpedoes at the *Chicago*. Both narrowly missed but one hit the harbour bottom, exploded and sank the *Kuttabul*, a former ferry being used as a store ship. Twenty seamen from the Royal Australian Navy were killed, while several others were severely wounded in what was the first and only enemy action in the harbour's history.

About 400 metres to the south of Fort Denison and to the east of Bennelong Point lies the beautifully symmetrical Farm Cove. The cove's sweeping curve, with its creamy stone sea wall, contains the Royal Botanic Gardens, bequeathed to the nation by Governor Phillip in one of his last administrative acts in 1792. The cove, with its kelp-covered wall, is a haven for all manner of marine life. I have seen seals there in winter and fairy penguins too. There are wild ducks and ibis, seagulls and sometimes even pelicans drawn by the tranquillity and the certainty that they will be fed by the visitors who stroll around its edge.

In 1816, Governor Lachlan Macquarie had a five-kilometre carriage road cut from Old Government House down along the bush-covered ridge that separates Farm Cove from Woolloomooloo Bay so that his wife, Elizabeth, could better enjoy the harbour view from what had become known as the Government Domain. On a sandstone bluff at the end of the promontory he had a large seat or couch carved so that Mrs Macquarie could rest. The stone seat can still be seen under the enormous overhanging arches of Port Jackson and Moreton Bay fig trees, and today the headland is officially known as Mrs Macquarie's Chair. The Domain, a glorious green parkland covering some 71 hectares, incorporates 26 hectares enclosed and reserved as the Botanic Gardens.

It was here, in 1954, that Queen Elizabeth II, at that time monarch for only a year, stepped ashore for the first time as Queen of Australia. Indeed, it was the first time in what was then 166 years of European settlement in Australia that a reigning British monarch had set foot on Australian soil. The spot, on the cove's eastern shore, is marked by a beautifully carved and engraved sandstone memorial.

Directly across the cove, on its far western flank and directly beneath the Opera House, is a flight of stone steps and a public landing known as Man O' War Steps. The jetty, originally under naval control, served as a landing site which provided officers and dignitaries with the most direct access to Government House. Over the decades the jetty was the scene of many important moments in early Australian history in the way of arrivals — and departures. It was here too in the 1850s that a stone cottage was constructed for the use of watermen who slung their hammocks inside, drew their pulling boats up on the little beach outside and waited to be roused by men and women wanting to cross the harbour. The beach is still there and on warm summer nights, when the air is still and that great sheet of water is lit by a glorious golden moon, I fancy I can still see the ghosts of the old boatmen, sitting out there by the seawall puffing their long white clay pipes while waiting for one more journey.

The Great Ferry Boat Race has become an exciting part of the annual Festival of Sydney. Crowded with revellers, the ferries compete over a harbour course for the sheer fun of it.

IBM
ROYAL INSURANCE
ESSO
TOURCOING

The Upper Harbour

When Captain Arthur Phillip chose Sydney Cove as the best of the bays to set up camp and so lay the colonial foundations for what was to become one of the world's great seaports, he had no idea that not much further than a stone's throw to the west, a much more splendid, vast and capacious harbour within the harbour lay in all its pristine glory. It was not until his men scrambled to the top of the steep and stony ridge high above the cove, to what is now Observatory Hill, that they saw on the other side, the incredible extent of the upper harbour. There, stretching away before them was an apparently endless maze of coves and bays and creeks, laid down like some fantastic silver-blue fern pinned upon the olive drab cloak of the bush.

It did not take long for the surveying Captain John Hunter, Master of the *Sirius*, to take a boat from Sydney Cove, around past what is now Walsh Bay, and swing south to find himself in a serenely tranquil stretch of water. There, growing thickly by the water's edge in the coarse black mud of the tidal flats he saw hectare upon hectare of golden reeds swaying on the nor'east wind which the Aboriginals called Toogara. Behind the reeds and on the shoreline was the distinctive green and gold of the wattle which, many years later, would come to symbolise the strength of the young nation's sporting prowess.

Both the reeds and the wattle were exceptionally important to the infant colony. The reeds were used to thatch the roofs of the convict huts whose walls were in turn crudely fashioned from ''wattle and daub'' . . . woven wattle laths plastered with mud. But perhaps more important than the materials for shelter which were to be found there, Hunter and his men also saw vast Aboriginal shell middens, sun-bleached and white like the graveyards of whales. The middens, millions of shells piled up over thousands of years, pointed to the crustacean riches that lay within the mudflats. Food, the scarcest of all commodities in those first dreadful years of privation and appalling hardship, was there for the taking. Which is why the harbour within the harbour quickly became known as Cockle Bay.

Home with her catch, a deep-sea trawler chugs up Walsh Bay, past the revamped Pier One, on her way to the fish markets at Blackwattle Bay.

(Previous page) In the 19th century, Darling Harbour's eastern shore resembled the edge of a gigantic saw as berth after berth protruded into the waterway. In the 1960s the old jetties were replaced.

(Right) Dwarfed by the sheer glass walls of the new Maritime Centre, an old brick bond store stands as a reminder of an era not long past.

It was a wonderfully evocative name which deserved to endure. Unfortunately, at least for the romantics among us, the name was changed to Darling Harbour in honour of Major-General Ralph Darling, who in the course of serving as colonial governor between 1823 and 1851, gave his name to half a dozen of the harbour's most prominent features. Darling Harbour was destined to become the commercial hub of the great port city. Less than a century after Governor Darling's departure, his namesake was home to no fewer than 50 berths crammed with ships from all nations, loading Australian wool and primary produce bound for Britain, Europe and North America and in return, discharging their manufactured goods. At the southern end of that long row of grey wooden jetties, on the site of the ancient mudflats and middens first seen by Hunter and his men, a great railway goods yard spread its rails like a steely spider's web. In the 1920s the yards sprawled over 22 hectares with a total of 50

Darling Harbour is not always packed with tourists. Contemplating a still summer's morning, one might almost hear the ghosts of long forgotten mariners pulling and hauling aboard the ships of the Sydney Maritime Museum.

Wilson Parking
SONY

kilometres of track handling four million tonnes of goods a year.

Today, the ancient face of Darling Harbour has been completely obliterated to make way for the most imaginative, the most ambitious and certainly the most expensive urban renewal project in the history of European settlement in Australia. The Darling Harbour Scheme, a multimillion-dollar facelift for the western waterfront, was initiated and indeed forced through over the wailing objections of environmentalists, historians, the media and lobbyists of all kinds. The New South Wales Labor Government's Premier, Neville Wran, and his controversial Minister for Public Works, Laurie Brereton, seized an unprecedented opportunity and to their everlasting credit, pulled off a triumph of urban planning, the biggest and most impressive public development in the bicentennial year.

Now, grouped around the impressive sweep of the bay are the glistening white-painted steel, glass and concrete monuments to Australian architectural ingenuity — the Convention Centre, the Exhibition Centre, the International Marketplace, the Aquarium and, most striking of all, the Australian National Maritime Museum. The museum sits on the water's edge, hard by the old Pyrmont Bridge (erected in 1858 as one of the colony's first toll bridges), its magnificent billowing white sails sheltering the central repository for the island nation's maritime heritage.

In the bicentennial year, the National Maritime Museum, perhaps more than any other single institution, was the recipient of special national gifts to mark Australia's historic maritime links with the wider world. One of the most generous gifts came from the United States Government in the form of a multimillion-dollar endowment to fund the establishment of a permanent US–Australia Gallery which traces our maritime relations from the very first contacts in 1789, marked by a whaler from Providence, Rhode Island, through the decisive Battle of the Coral Sea, the turning point in the Pacific War, to the present commercial and military links.

Like a gigantic spaceship poised for takeoff, Sydney's Centrepoint Tower rears above the silver stacks of the old Pyrmont Power Station.

The two concrete finger wharves that jut out from the towering steel and glass curves of the museum are home to some of the finest historic vessels in Australia. *Akarana*, the New Zealand Government's exceptionally generous bicentennial gift, is a plank-on-edge cutter from yachting's halcyon days when sailors carried on fearlessly in vastly overcanvassed boats of all shapes and sizes.

I found her, a salty, barnacle-encrusted wreck full of bird droppings, cracks and kelp, on the Parramatta River mudflats, a boat fit, if the truth be told, only for burning. But there was something graceful, almost spiritual, about her long, low, sleek lines that even the wear and tear and the years of sad neglect could not hide. Under all that dilapidation, the lines of a great champion, a thoroughbred, were impossible to disguise. I reseached her history and found magnificent photographs of her in my own collection of historic plate

The Darling Harbour redevelopment provided the impetus for the construction of Sydney's monorail. Although it arouses heated debate among city people, there can be no doubting its popularity with tourists.

glass negatives, subsequently donated to the National Maritime Museum. I then set about the task of finding someone with the will and above all the financial resources to restore her as a national treasure. The man who deserves much of the credit for her salvation is merchant banker Michael Fay, chairman of the New Zealand Bicentennial Committee and an ardent yachtsman who was then in Fremantle at the head of his extremely powerful first America's Cup challenge. Fay led me to her saviour in Wellington — New Zealand's Prime Minister, David Lange.

Lange loves boats and like all Kiwis, he also loves the idea of beating the Aussies. Which is probably why he fell in love with the idea of acquiring *Akarana*, taking her home for restoration and presenting her as New Zealand's bicentennial gift.

Built on Auckland's North Shore by Robert Logan, the white-bearded Grand Old Man of New Zealand naval architecture, *Akarana* and her Kiwi crew, which included old man Logan himself, came across the Tasman in 1888 with the sole intention of walloping their Aussie cousins and in the process cleaning up both in prizes and in the considerable cash wagers and side bets which were then accepted as an essential part of yachting. Sporting a colossal spread of canvas on a boom at least as long as the boat itself, *Akarana*, a renowned light air flier, astonished all the colonial cracks by winning both the Centennial Regattas in Sydney and Melbourne that year.

Today, beautifully restored by Auckland's wooden boat maestro, John Salthouse, she provides us all with a glimpse of a time when yachts were both fast and beautiful. David Lange no doubt still chuckles at the thought of Australian taxpayers forever footing the bill to commemorate their own defeat at the hands of the Kiwi flier.

Among the other historic vessels at the museum's wharves is the glorious old *Kathleen Gillett*, perhaps the most famous ocean-going vessel Australia has produced. Although only 50 years old, she was designed more than a century ago by the remarkable Norwegian (but of Scottish heritage) naval architect, Colin Archer, who in 1850 came to Australia with his brothers to seek their fortunes on the goldfields. Although they found no gold, the Archer brothers did become pioneer pastoralists in northern Queensland, where the Archer River is named for them. Colin Archer went home to Norway when his father died, but his brothers remained to run what became an enormously successful beef cattle property near Rockhampton.

Meanwhile, back in Larvik on Norway's beautiful but treacherously rocky south coast, Colin Archer perfected the lines of his world-famous double-enders which were to be incorporated half a century later in the design for the *Kathleen Gillett*, the second Australian flag-carrying vessel to circumnavigate the world. (The honour of being the first Australians to circumnavigate the globe fell to Harold Nossiter and his sons aboard the schooner *Sirius* in 1935.)

Kathleen Gillett was built in Looking Glass Bay at Drummoyne by the Swedish master craftsman, Charles Larsen, for the celebrated marine artist, Jack Earl. Earl and his wife, Kathleen, for whom the boat was named, dreamed of undertaking the first Australian circumnavigation. But although the yacht's keel was laid down in 1933, her construction extended over six long years.

Her launch in 1939 coincided with Hitler's attack on Poland, which immediately placed at least a temporary restraint on the Earls' world-wandering. But in 1945, immediately after the war and at a time when Australians were looking for the kind of inspiration that would lift them out of the emotional and physical doldrums, Jack Earl proposed the novel idea of a 600-nautical mile ocean race from Sydney to Hobart and in the process founded what is today one of the world's great bluewater classics. *Kathleen Gillett* was among the handful of boats that struggled down the coast in the inaugural fleet that set sail from Sydney Harbour on Boxing Day 1945.

(Right) A kaleidoscope of colour cascades down on Darling Harbour during Australia Day celebrations. January 26 marks the founding of the nation.

NZI
NZI
ESANDA

ROYAL
IBM
IBM
ESSO
HILTON

Crowds throng Darling Harbour's western promenade in front of the International Marketplace. Beyond, the white roof of the National Maritime Museum rises like billowing sails on a square-rigged ship.

(Previous page) The simple, functional shapes of the Georgian buildings on the eastern tip of Goat Island offer a vivid contrast to the city's thrusting, high-rise towers.

Her circumnavigation, a voyage which remains one of the great sea epics, took place between 1947 and 1948. She was subsequently sold and spent the following 40 years wandering around the Pacific Islands in the hands of plantation owners and crocodile shooters. In 1988 I found her sadly neglected on a mooring off the island of Guam in Micronesia, and convinced the Norwegian Ambassador to Australia, Per Haugestad, and through him the Norwegian Foreign Minister, Thorvald Stoltenberg, that the Oslo government should acquire her and bring her home to Sydney for restoration and presentation to the Australian people through the National Maritime Museum.

The Norwegian Government, with I suspect more than a little encouragement from Norway's great sailing monarch, King Olaf, and his son, Crown Prince Harald, agreed to fund the restoration which was carried out by Sydney's greatest wooden boat builders, the Norwegian-born Halvorsens, at Bobbin Head. The entire restoration was under the command of one of Australia's most skilful craftsmen, Trevor Gowland, a brilliant sailor and America's Cup veteran, who has a reputation second to none when it comes to understanding the ways of wooden boats.

Kathleen Gillett was brought home through the generosity of Israel's Zim Line and presented to the National Maritime Museum as a lasting tribute to the friendship and the maritime historic links between the Norwegian and Australian people.

The National Maritime Museum was designed by Australia's foremost architect, Philip Cox, who also created Darling Harbour's futuristic Exhibition Centre. Darling Harbour, with its huge Convention Centre and International Marketplace, its Chinese Gardens and vast open spaces right by the water's edge, has become a mecca for tourists and city residents alike.

But Darling Harbour is much more than simply a playground. It remains very much part of the working port. Although the delightful old wooden finger wharves along its eastern shore have long since given way to modern and not at all attractive concrete strip berths backed by ugly prefabricated concrete storage sheds, hundreds of thousands of tonnes of cargo, much of it softwood from North America, roll-on, roll-off containerised freight from Europe and New Zealand, streams of cars from Japan, and much else besides continue to come ashore there every year.

At the northern end of Darling Harbour, standing tall like a gigantic concrete phallus, is the glass-topped tower that houses the Maritime Services Board's harbour traffic control staff. Peering through their green-tinted glass, the controllers maintain radio contact with all in-bound and seagoing vessels, carefully judging time and distance so that they never have huge ships swinging in and out of tight harbour turns at the same potentially calamitous moment. Nicknamed "the Pill" (because it controls all berths in the harbour), the tower also plays a vital role in co-ordinating tugs and pilots.

To the west of Darling Harbour, the Upper Harbour dips in and out of several businesslike bays with colourful or workmanlike and practical names like Pyrmont and Blackwattle Bay, Johnston's Bay and White Bay, all serve to feed the industrial heart of the city. The Pyrmont wharves, once the scene of constant comings and goings by large overseas passenger liners and busy freighters, now lie mostly idle. Although most of the container traffic now moves through the modern terminals at Port Botany, the great concrete apron at White Bay with its towering overhead gantry cranes continues to play an important part in the container trade.

In March 1942 the old wooden wharves at Glebe Island saw the disembarkation of some 8400 American troops — the first large contingent of US servicemen to arrive in Australia, in transit to the war zones of the Pacific. The American troops, who embarked at Boston, came to Sydney aboard the *Queen Mary*, but the great liner was too big to pass safely under the Harbour Bridge. She remained on a mooring at Athol Bight while the troops were ferried up the harbour to Glebe Island and the rail links which were to take them to staging camps outside the city.

Beyond White Bay to the west and up under the unlovely span of Glebe Island Bridge lie the timber berths of Rozelle Bay. Although the origins of the name Rozelle are obscure, the bay — which has some of the deepest water west of the Harbour Bridge — is believed to have taken its name from the schooner *Rozelle*, built there in the late 19th century and wrecked off Narrabeen in 1914. Here, massive logs from New Zealand, New Guinea, Canada and North America lie half-submerged in the scummy water, cheek by kelp-bearded jowl with dun-coloured floating containers crammed with the finest flitches of oregon and spruce.

Immediately to the east lies Blackwattle Bay, also one of the deepest bays on the harbour's southern shore. In its inner recesses in the earliest years of European settlement, hunting parties came ashore to shoot game in what was known as the Kangaroo Grounds. Today, the most distinctive feature of Blackwattle Bay is the fish markets, a rowdy, odoriferous, multilingual melting pot where Italian and now Vietnamese fishermen rub shoulders with Greeks and Lebanese and Irish-Australians in a glorious cacophony of buying and selling. The fish markets, controlled by the NSW Fish Marketing Authority, have an annual turnover in excess of $60 million and although much of the fresh seafood these days comes from offshore grounds, the harbour still yields an enormous quantity of prawns and bream, tailor and sweet, tasty little leatherjackets.

Think of seafood and Sydney Harbour and one immediately thinks of the name Doyle. The Doyle family have been fishermen since the earliest days of convict settlement. Their earliest forebear in Australia was the convict, Henry Newton, who, with his brothers, hauled the seine on the harbour from their own boats, supplying the growing needs of the settlement at Sydney Cove. The Newtons were apparently very good fishermen. So much so that, in 1883, members of the wealthy Fairfax family who owned the *Sydney Morning Herald*, not only went out fishing with them but loaned them what was then the considerable sum of £60 to purchase the waterfront property at Watson's Bay which is today the site of Australia's best-known seafood restaurant. Henry Newton, the illiterate fisherman who with a strong hand made his mark — X — on the original property documents, founded what has become the Doyle dynasty. Under the guidance first of matriarch Alice and now her son, Peter, Doyle's On The Beach, the quaint little Watson's Bay cottage once known as the Ozone and which was cobbled together from second-hand building materials hauled down the harbour from Point Piper, has become synonymous with the finest in fresh seafood.

Peter Doyle, fisherman and restaurateur, buys at the Blackwattle Bay fish markets.

(Right) Sydney's water police maintain a constant vigilance. Descendant from a convict rowboat guard, the unit is equipped with high-speed launches.

(Overleaf) A ro-ro vessel, named for its roll-on, roll-off ramp tucked up astern, makes her way down Walsh Bay, past the city's northern fringe toward the Harbour Bridge.

The family tradition demands an intimate knowledge of everything that swims in the sea, which is why Peter Doyle can be seen in his gumboots and apron at the Blackwattle Bay fish markets every morning at dawn, examining the catch, humping cartons and crates and buying for the three Sydney Harbour restaurants that now bear the family name.

POLICE

AMP
GOLD FIELDS
BARCLAYS

ROYALE
ROYALE

Balmain and

the Islands

I GREW UP ON THE WATERFRONT at the eastern end of the Balmain peninsula in those far-off days before it became the almost exclusive preserve of media mega-trendies, advertising gurus and real estate sharks. My Balmain East of the 1950s was a village, plain and simple — Mrs Hawkins' Post Office, two tiled pubs, the Commercial and the Shipwright's Arms, Eva Spencer's cake shop, Ronny Blunden, the butcher, Dick Chieu, the Chinese grocer, and Horrie Burke's paper shop. Not an antique dealer or a croissant within cooee. It was a real neighbourhood, small, close-knit, the kind of place where families knew each other over several generations and for the most part, got on well. The men worked on the waterfront and their wives were either bound up with domesticity or out at work in one of the many factories in the area.

The East End, like a stubby nail, somehow disembodied at the end of the long index finger of the peninsula, existed in almost defiant independence. It was a community which, as Ruth Park found out when she toured Balmain's 28 pubs, proudly admitted to only one alma mater: Balmain. ''Yeah,'' a drinker, with a superior air, in one of the old pubs told her, ''one of these days Balmain may join the Commonwealth. But I dunno. We're still chewing over whether we'll join New South.''

Down at the East End, that sense of them and us was even more pronounced. We were somehow glad to be cut off. There was the faithful old tram, of course, rattling its way up Darling Street with a couple of ramshackle old carriages reluctantly clattering along behind. The tram connected us East Enders with Balmain proper, down that long slippery dip of a hill and then creeping like a snail, up the other side, past the Pigeon Ground (Gladstone Park) before we reached Saturday's holy of holies, The Hoyts and the great Victorian bulk of the Town Hall. There, since trams were incapable of 90 degree turns, it was all-change for the city-bound tram that rumbled up from Birchgrove.

The solitary joy of single-handed sailing can be no less rewarding to any skipper alone on the harbour than it is to a Kay Cottee or an Ian Kiernan.

(Right) Galvanised roofs at Mort's Bay offer a mosaic. The bay's Victorian architecture is complemented now by modern homes.

(Previous page) Cheek by rusty jowl, timber freighters lie snug at the dolphins in Snail's Bay while sunset creeps over the western reaches of the harbour.

At Balmain East the trams started at the very water's edge, right down the bottom of Darling Street Wharf. The hill behind the wharf was so impossibly steep that a huge black and gold striped counterweight — the dummy, we called it — had to be hooked onto the trams to haul them with a shudder and a groan up to the summit.

I preferred to go by ferry. Every half hour or so, Nicholson Bros ferries (later taken over by Stannards), the *Proclaim*, *Produce*, *Provide*, *Promote* (their names all prefixed for some mysterious reason with *Pro*), chugged into rickety old Darling Street Wharf with its huge curved iron waiting shed, all dark and dank and stinking of pigeons and port wine. They took a handful of passengers to the city's back door, Erskine Street. It was not until the early 1970s that Balmainites were permitted to catch a ferry to the city's front door, the Quay. As an adolescent socialist, I imagined that that (like the fact that we were on the dark side of the Bridge) was somehow con-

(Above) Although Goat Island's 5.5 hectares consist chiefly of exceptionally fine quality sandstone, its rocky hilltop nevertheless boasts trees and verdant pastures which not long ago provided grazing for sheep.

(Left) The Dawn Fraser Baths, named for Australia's most honoured Olympic champion, are tucked into White Horse Point at Balmain, a stone's throw from the house in which the swimmer has spent all her life.

(Previous page) The western sun leaves the bleak industrial landscape at Balmain's White Bay in silhouette, masking the busiest part of the port area's grain, coal and container handling facilities.

nected with The Powers That Be keeping the wharfie suburb's working class in their place.

As kids we hitched our dinghies to the big bronze bollard aft on the ferry's sponson, whooshing our way across Darling Harbour like maniacal young Ahabs towed in a welter of spray behind the Great White Whale. The legendary Balmain identity, "Wee Georgie" Robinson, the tiny man with the towering sporting reputation (Balmain footballer, 18-footer champion) told me how, during the Great Depression, he had been out in his 18ft rowing skiff collecting floating coke and firewood in Darling Harbour when a huge grey nurse shark, at least as big as his boat, followed him all the way home to Balmain East, like a faithful dog.

In all those years in Balmain, swimming in the harbour virtually every day, we never gave a second thought to sharks — although one of the great local legends from the early '50s concerned a young man who dived off the wharf near the hot water outlet at the old Balmain Power House, and who was supposed to have plunged directly down the throat of a giant white pointer. One gulp and he was gone, we were told. It never made a scrap of difference to our swimming around the Balmain waterfront.

We built rafts and tin canoes and dinghies fashioned from canvas and plywood and anything else we could scrounge around the waterfront. The East End of Balmain was within shouting distance of the forbidden Goat Island, the Maritime Services Board base. Landing there, on the little white sandy beach on the western shore, was like coming ashore with Silver and that murderous crew on our very own Treasure Island.

There were blue swimmer crabs and mussels and oysters and bream for the taking. A line, a prawn, or even a lump of mouldy old cheese were all that was necessary.

Ruth Park caught the atmosphere of the old suburb when she wrote that "the houses are squeezed amongst pubs, corner shops, factories, shipyards and metal works. The sea shows in bright blue slivers through lattices and around chimneypots; it lives at the end of every canted street, not openly so, as in Mosman, but seen through the interstices of masts, winches, chimneys, rigging. The whole suburb lives with ships and the sea. This uniquely natural, joyful atmosphere is Balmain's own."

Well, it was Balmain's own. But that was long ago. One by one the waterfront industries, the ship repair yards, the docks, the sailmakers' lofts and the tugboat bases closed down or moved away and the Balmain we used to joke about as "the Garden Suburb" did indeed begin to regenerate. Workers' cottages were snapped up by the middle-class young, eager to be in a less expensive version of trendy Paddington and close to the city. Old houses that had not seen a lick of paint in 20 years suddenly looked trim and neat. People actually planted trees, with the result that those mean little streets where the black tar bubbled in the summer heat, were cooled by unaccustomed shade. Balmain was reborn after a fashion. The grime is gone but, in truth, I much preferred it the way it was.

At the southern end of the Balmain peninsula and at the head of Johnston's Bay, lies Peacock Point (named not as one might suppose for the beautiful birds but for some otherwise anonymous Circular Quay wharfinger of the 1840s). There too is the Illoura Reserve, a delightful strip of green lawn with native scrub and casuarina trees and a long stone seawall where sweet, prickly-skinned leatherjackets are still hauled out of the harbour shallows by little boys with barbed spears. At the northern end lies Simmons Point, and another small reserve directly opposite Goat Island. Although there is a good depth of water here in what is known as The Needles, the island is barely 200 metres from the point and as a result the tidal race can often be ferocious.

Balmain takes its name from William Balmain, the only one of the eight First Fleet surgeons (apart from Surgeon John White of White Bay) to have his memory thus perpetuated. A Scot from Perthshire, Balmain was just 26 when he arrived in Sydney aboard

Wright's Point at Drummoyne. Here, harbourside homes often come with tennis courts and boat ramps.
(Left) Why is Sydney the most beautiful city in the world? A picture is more eloquent than a thousand words.
(Overleaf) Dobroyd Point shelters many of Sydney's small professional fishing boats.

the *Alexander*, the largest of the convict transports. He served with distinction both in Sydney and for four years on Norfolk Island and became Principal Surgeon in NSW. Over the years, Balmain made quite a fortune through the sale of imported rum and tea. He was awarded land grants on the Hawkesbury and at Field of Mars, on the Parramatta River. In April 1800 his friend, Governor Hunter, gave him the entire Balmain peninsula, all 222 hectares.

The peninsula had been passed over by many others seeking grants and by all accounts it was thought of as being not much of a gift. A steep-sided ridge ran up the spine of the peninsula, which was dominated by wild scrub and rock with very little topsoil. But the wily Balmain had no intention of living there, let alone cultivating the land. Instead, it seems he may have procured the grant with the sole purpose of disposing of it almost immediately to a Calcutta merchant, John Gilchrist, in payment for a cargo which Gilchrist delivered to London in Balmain's name. To complete the transaction, Balmain sold the peninsula to Gilchrist for five shillings in 1801 and sailed for London soon afterwards. Gilchrist held the grant for 30 years before he subdivided, pushed The Balmain Road (Darling Street) through to Parramatta Road and sold it for £50,000.

When the first of the new-fangled steamships began arriving in Sydney in the 1850s, Thomas Sutcliffe Mort, one of the young colony's most adventurous entrepreneurs, seized the opportunity to construct Sydney's first dockyard on a four-hectare site he purchased in Waterview Bay, Balmain. At that time, Sydney was awash with disappointed diggers who had exhausted their luck on the goldfields and who had returned to Sydney desperate for work. Mort hired them and put them to work excavating, with pick and shovel, a dock 120 metres long and 15 metres wide, in the solid sandstone. Mort's Dock was to become a Sydney landmark, not least because it supplied half of Balmain with fresh fish every time it took in a ship and pumped itself dry. It docked its first ship, the coastal steamer, *Hunter*, in 1855 and soon employed a workforce of 700 men, not only at the dock but in associated shipbuilding, engineering and boilermaking activities that grew up around it in Balmain. In the later years of the 19th century, Balmain's impossibly narrow streets were lined with ranks of tiny, narrow-gutted terrace houses that marched cheek-by-jowl down to the harbour, providing accommodation for a working population that at one stage exceeded that of any other part of Sydney.

The old Mort's Dock is gone now, but the State government has spent millions of dollars turning the site into a magnificent harbourside park. In fact, Balmain probably has more parks than most other Sydney suburbs. Birchgrove Park, once mudflats at the head of Snail's Bay, is one of the least interesting even if it is one of the biggest. A much more interesting park is perched not far away, right at the very tip of Long Nose Point. There, like the Illoura Reserve on Peacock Point, some effort has been made to maintain what is left of the natural landform. The multilevel park was the site of Morrison and Sinclair's shipyard and it was here that some of Sydney's most famous racing yachts including the great Sydney–Hobart racer, *Morna*, were built.

Louisa Road (aptly termed Lousy Road by its residents) winds its narrow and impossibly crowded way down the spine of Long Nose Point. The late Victorian terraces on either side have glorious waterfrontages or at the very least, spectacular waterviews. Until recently, many of them were the homes of boatbuilders and craftsmen associated with the shipbuilding industry. Only a handful of the old-timers remain. One of them is Arthur Griffith, a master at ships' joinery and a veteran boatbuilder whose tiny terrace house tumbles down to a ramshackle old boatshed on the water's edge where for two years he laboured daily on the restoration of the *Britannia*, the most famous of all the old Sydney Harbour 18-footers. Griffith's great skill and his painstaking attention to detail brought the old red cedar hull back to life. Built in 1918, "the Brit", as she was known throughout the harbour, raced for 25 years with a crew of 15 Balmain footballers under "Wee Georgie" Robinson. She then served a further 25 years as a starter's boat, a record never likely to be equalled in Sydney or anywhere else. *Britannia* will never sail again, although her gear, all 280 square metres of it, again awes all those who see her fully rigged and on display in the Great Hall at the Australian National Maritime Museum in Darling Harbour.

Opposite Long Nose Point, barely 300 metres away on the northern shore, lies the bushland of the Ball's Head Reserve, named for Henry Lidgbird Ball, the naval officer commanding HMS *Supply*. Below that great stone bluff, the harbour floor suddenly dips down to its deepest point. To the east lies Berry's Bay, another famous boatbuilding site and now home to huge oil storage tanks. It was in Berry's Bay that the legendary Billy Barnett, the great master boatbuilder who became one of the most feared skippers on the harbour, built Australia's second America's Cup challenger, *Dame Pattie*. There are more gigantic oil tanks, spectacular only in their ugliness, across Ball's Head Bay on the northern shore of Gore Cove near Mann's Point. Eventually, all these industrial sites will, it is hoped, be moved south to Botany Bay, opening the waterfront sites up for public recreational purposes and/or homes.

Westward from Greenwich Point, the harbour divides itself into two separate arms. On the starboard side, to the right of Woolwich, the lovely Lane Cove River (named because in 1788 it reminded Phillip of a winding, wooded country lane) snakes around some of the most magnificent waterfront properties in the upper harbour as it laps past Woodford Bay, Tambourine Bay and Burns Bay, embracing the northern shore of historic Hunter's Hill and Longueville. Commanding the heights above the languid river is the great stone pile of St Ignatius College at Riverview.

On the port hand, below Woolwich, the Parramatta River begins its many tortuous twists and turns, winding all the way up to what is now the City of Parramatta. Cockatoo Island splits the Parramatta River into two arms, one flowing past the Balmain shore and the other around by the southern shore of Hunter's Hill.

Cockatoo's 16 hectares, with its two graving docks, a floating dock and extensive workshops, is the biggest shipyard in Sydney and the biggest of the harbour's eight islands. In his history of Cockatoo Island, Captain Roger Parker writes that until 1839, the great outcrop of sandstone was covered by a tall red-gum forest inhabited by thousands of the brilliant white sulphur-crested cockatoos for which it was named.

After that year, Cockatoo replaced Goat Island as a prison for recidivist convicts. The island was notorious for the severity of its regime, its short-lived but ferocious mutinies and the many attempts at escape. The writer, Louis Becke, who as a boy lived at Woolwich, described how he and his brother listened, on foggy days, for "the muffled clamour of that dreadful bell and the sound of someone panting hard in his swim for liberty. One winter's day, a wretched creature was found clinging with bleeding hands to the oyster-covered rocks beneath our house, too weak to drag himself further from his pursuers."

(Left) Veiled in early morning drizzle, a ferry takes commuters from Drummoyne, past Spectacle Island and on into Circular Quay and their city offices.

In 1863 however, Frederick Ward did succeed in swimming from the Cockatoo Island prison. Ward subsequently earned himself a notorious niche in Australian history as the bushranger known and feared as Captain Thunderbolt. Governor Gipps set the convicts to work on the island's sandstone heart, quarrying no less than 20 bottle-shaped silos for the storage of wheat.

But if the history of Cockatoo is tinged with sadness, spare a thought for the men who were cast ashore on Goat Island, the harbour's most notorious prison. Working in irons, even under the relatively humane Governor Bourke, the Goat Island convicts were forced to quarry stone under appalling conditions.

Of all the stories of that ghastly convict past, surely none is more terrible than that of Charles ''Bony'' Anderson, born in a London workhouse in 1816, apprenticed in a collier at nine and transported for seven years in 1834 for his part in a drunken brawl in which a shop window was broken.

Anderson was illiterate, spoke ''thick as a beast, should a beast speak'', and bore a depressed scar from a head wound received in battle during his years with the Royal Navy. What Anderson did have, however, was an unbreakable spirit, despite the unbelievable punishment he suffered. His term at Goat Island was marked by a monotonous record of floggings for heinous crimes like . . . staring at a passing steamer.

Despite the shark-infested waters around the island, he tried to escape many times and each time he was caught, brought back and flogged. Finally judged to be an intractable felon, he was chained to a rock and left out in the open for two years.

There, with a crude hammer and chisel, he carved a sandstone couch for himself. It's still there, perhaps the most poignant monument of all to the horrors of Australia's convict past. Anderson's chain was eight metres long and attached to trumpet irons on his legs. With maggots feasting on the open wounds on his back, he came to resemble a hideous Caliban, a monster so wild and unapproachable that his food was pushed out to him by his guards at the end of a long pole.

Under a penalty of 100 lashes his fellow convicts were forbidden to speak or even to look at him. When rain fell he wallowed in muddy puddles, bellowing like a bullock. The free settlers who had taken up waterfront plots at the east end of Balmain finally petitioned the governor to end his misery, not because they were moved by the man's plight but because his wailing lamentations disturbed their sensibilities if not their slumbers.

Three other islands are visible from White Horse Point on the Balmain shore. They are Snapper Island, Spectacle Island and further up the river toward Henley, Rodd Island. Like Cockatoo, Snapper Island is Commonwealth property and although the naval presence there is being deliberately run down, it remains home to Sydney's Sea Cadet Corps. Spectacle Island is another Federal government property, which has long been used as a naval armament storage depot. Rodd Island sits low and snug in Iron Cove. Like Shark and Clarke Islands in the main harbour, Rodd Island is essentially a picnic place. It is open to the public upon request to the National Parks and Wildlife authorities.

A four launches its craft from the St Ignatius College shed in Tambourine Bay.

(Left) Berry's Bay continues a long tradition of association with maritime craftsmanship. Boatbuilding, engineering and ship repair facilities have lined its shores since the 1870s.

(Pages 82–83) Traditional wooden boat building is not entirely the lost art many imagine. In Balmain, the grand tradition of carvel planking, with its painstaking caulking and red-leading, goes on in defiance of fibreglass.

The

Northern Side

BRADLEY'S HEAD IS ONE OF THE harbour's most prominent headlands. It remains a magnificent memorial to the memory of William Bradley, a first lieutenant aboard the First Fleet's flagship, the armed tender HMS *Sirius*, and the man whose beautifully illustrated and clearly penned journal provides such a vivid portrait of the beginnings of European settlement in Sydney. Bradley landed there with Captain John Hunter, two days after the Union flag was raised at Sydney Cove. Bradley's journal, remarkable for its meticulous observations and recordings, provides us with a complete account of the harbour's first exploration and surveys by water. A keen observer of plants and animals and of the Aboriginal people, it was, he says, his melancholy duty to carry out Governor Phillip's orders to capture white Australia's first black prisoners, Benallon (Bennelong) and Colbee, "by far the most unpleasant service I ever was ordered to Execute".

Bradley's Head stands at the southernmost tip of Ashton Park, 50 hectares of beautiful natural bushland in which the mighty twisted trunks of pink angophoras still grow on impossible sandstone ledges right by the saltwater's edge. Like much of the harbour's bush-clad foreshores, Bradley's Head owes its existence largely to the strategic concerns, not to say paranoias of the settlement's 19th century military commanders. In 1841 it was decided to turn Bradley's Head into a fortress. A huge gun pit was cut into the solid sandstone on top of the headland and a thick defensive stone wall was thrown up around it. But the construction work was no sooner completed than it was abandoned. In faraway Westminster, the authorities responsible for paying for it all suddenly decided they could no longer afford it.

The fort was all but abandoned for 30 years. In 1871, three gun pits, a powder magazine and a stone gallery were completed. As Ruth Park points out, the stone fortifications were much in demand by late 19th century photographers who either rowed across from the Quay or trekked down through narrow bush tracks to pose their crinolined womenfolk against them in the same way their English contemporaries draped their women against Roman columns. Snippets from 19th century diaries tell of some of the hazards and not a few of the delights of going by boat . . . "tremendous squall from the south . . . torrents of rain . . . large hailstones . . . muttonchops soon fried on forked sticks . . . crackle of campfire . . . various cries of animals". Other photographers who struggled overland wrote of . . . "high broken ground . . . mosquitoes, also battalions of light infantry (fleas) . . . and a few steps bring one from the depths of the bush to the verge of the precipice, another step would precipitate him into the fearful gulf that yawns beneath!"

Hope springs eternal for the harbour's amateur fishermen and not least for those who cast their lines from the rocks at the base of Bradley's Head.

(Right) Clinging limpet-like to the sandstone, a glorious angophora overlooks the shallow green tranquility of Taylors Bay.

(Previous page) Lavender Bay. Long before the Bridge bypassed it, the bay was a busy depot for farm produce brought by horse and cart from the farms of the North Shore. Punts took the carts across to Dawes Point.

In 1978, the Australian Heritage Commission gazetted Bradley's Head as part of the National Estate. It is also an integral part of Sydney Harbour National Park, a body of bushland of several hundred hectares, much of it in pristine condition, which stretches from the salt-blasted heathlands atop North Head, very nearly all the way around the northern shoreline.

On a sandstone ledge at the very tip of Bradley's Head, stands the steel-grey fighting top from HMAS *Sydney*, commemorating her victory over the German raider, the battlecruiser *Emden*. Nearby, on another ledge by the water's edge stands a solitary sandstone pillar which marks one end of the nautical mile measured from the martello tower on Fort Denison. The Doric column once adorned the old George Street post office which predated the present GPO in Martin Place.

West from Bradley's Head is the broad sweep of Athol Bay, often referred to as Athol Bight, one of the safest deepwater anchorages in the harbour. It was here, during the Second World War that the giant liners, *Queen Elizabeth* and *Queen Mary*, too big to steam up the harbour and under the bridge, swung on moorings to discharge their tens of thousands of troops.

Above Athol Bay's green and wooded slopes stands what is arguably the world's best-sited zoo. Taronga (the ancient Aboriginal word means water view) Park commands a multimillion-dollar view to virtually all parts of the main harbour from the Heads to Sydney Cove. The zoo, founded in 1881 and established on the slopes of Mosman in 1916, was originally located on three hectares of land known as the Billygoat Swamp at Moore Park. But because its collections and its popularity grew and grew, it was moved to what was then the more spacious site on the harbour's northern shore. The Mosman site was an inspired choice. I know of no other zoo anywhere in the world where animals and visitors alike enjoy such a splendid natural setting.

The next cove to the westward of Athol Bight is Little Sirius Cove, named for the First Fleet flagship which made its heroic 219-day voyage to Cape Town for the supplies that rescued the tiny settlement from the brink of starvation in 1789. It was in Great Sirius Cove (now generally known as Mosman Bay) that the *Sirius*, weary with months of weed and barnacle growth on her wooden hull, was careened and scraped clean. That laborious task, which took four months, was undertaken after an exhaustive survey by Lieutenant Bradley who determined the best position for the ship's anchors to be dug in and shore braces and lines rigged so that she could be heaved down and worked on. Those lines came ashore almost exactly where Mosman Bay ferry wharf now stands.

While the ship was being careened, two members of her crew were lost in the bush for three days and on another occasion, one of her midshipmen, Francis Hill, vanished into the bush and was never seen again although the ship's guns were fired at four-hourly intervals for several days. After her refit, *Sirius* sailed to Norfolk Island where she was wrecked without loss of life in March 1790.

The name Mosman Bay and indeed the harbourside suburb of Mosman, derives from Archibald Mosman who established a whaling station (and a stinking try works) there in 1830. Mosman built a large stone pier, a spacious home for himself which he named The Nest and two smaller stone cottages for his ships' officers and their crews. One of Mosman's two stone storehouses, its doorway flanked by two large whalebones, has survived to become home to a Mosman Scout group.

When Mosman sold out and moved to a New England grazing property in 1839 (just before the collapse of the whaling industry), the Mosman estate was sold to Richard Harnett, yachtsman, designer and one of the North Shore's great entrepreneurs and promoters. It was Harnett, a foundation member of the Royal Sydney Yacht Squadron, who first conceived the notion of an Australian America's Cup challenge and who in 1858 designed "the famous little Australian" along the lines of a mackerel he caught and dissected in Woolloomooloo Bay. From such an unlikely source emerged a wildly overcanvassed cutter, *The Australian*, which was among the fastest, most spectacular and most successful yachts to race on the harbour during the 19th century.

Still waters run deep. That is certainly the case in Little Sirius Cove where the rocky shore plunges suddenly into exceptionally clear water sufficiently deep to accommodate the biggest yachts on the harbour.

(Overleaf) Mosman Bay's famous rowing club sits surrounded by racing yachts and cruising boats. The bay, once dominated by the sights and smells of whaling, is home for one of the harbour's biggest fleets of small craft.

TEN
SPORTS!

Much of Shell Cove is fringed by a park that guarantees public access to the harbour. The cove is named for the Aboriginal middens used by convicts to make lime.

(Left) Neutral Bay's eastern shore and beyond it tranquil Shell Cove and the blue Pacific. In 1789, the bay was set aside as an anchorage for ships from nations declared neutral in Britain's war with France.

The white-bearded Harnett somehow got rid of the smell of rendered whale blubber and turned the old Mosman whaling station into a pleasure resort with paddlewheeler ferries bringing people for picnics, pigeon shooting, coconut shies, lovers' lanes and Crowe's Celebrated Quadrille Band. Harnett ran two ferries to and from the Quay. The venture went bust, Harnett sold and 12 years later, repurchased the property.

At the turn of the century, Mosman's bushland was to be immortalised by the famous artists' camp established at the water's edge by some of Australia's great painters including Julian Ashton, Tom Roberts, and Arthur Streeton.

In their beautifully illustrated book, *Sydney Harbour, Paintings Since 1794*, Sandra McGrath and Robert Walker report that the artists chose to live in such camps for a variety of reasons, not least because they provided an open and free lifestyle. "For a pound a week," according to McGrath and Walker, "an artist could enjoy breathtaking views of the harbour, be close to the rocky, natural bushland and have easy access to the city." Many of Arthur Streeton's greatest works were painted around his camp at Sirius Cove.

In a letter to his friend Tom Roberts, Streeton captures the romantically evocative mood of the harbour in the 19th century. "I lay on the [ferry's] paddlebox coming home from Manly last night and the soft, dark breath of the harbour playing through my hair . . . All seemed like a dream . . . Just like a long, sad, soothing melody."

The artists' camp in Sirius Cove has recently been "rediscovered" and tidied up. Cremorne Point, now crowded with home units and apartment blocks, still has many fine old homes with incomparable harbour views and is also one of those marvellous places, unfortunately all too rare in Sydney, where a high population density is made to seem not quite so overwhelming by complete public access to virtually all the foreshores.

In 1816, Governor Thomas Brisbane gave the entire peninsula to James Robertson, the astronomer sent from London to take charge of the Parramatta Observatory. In 1853 Robertson sold the peninsula to James Milson (of Milson's Point) who in turn leased it to two theatrical promoters who cleared the bushy ridge, laid down tracks and established gardens and built a jetty. They offered a quadrille band, a huge dancing stage and a merry-go-round for children. There was archery, rifle-shooting and fireworks at night. But the pleasure grounds, named after the notorious Cremorne Gardens in Regency London, lasted only six years. The waterfront land was then to be chopped up and sold off for quick profit. But in 1891 the government intervened to block the sale and in the process decreed that a stretch of waterfrontage, two kilometres long and with a depth of 30 metres from the highwater mark should remain public property. The landmark decision saved the bush-clad waterfront in Mosman Bay and Shell Cove.

One of the few buildings actually on the water's edge in Mosman Bay is the delightful little weatherboard cottage and boatshed home of the Sydney Amateur Sailing Club, one of Australia's oldest and most distinguished yacht clubs. Founded in 1872, the Amateurs' original clubhouse, a two-storey wooden boatshed topped by a bold white flagstaff, stood not far from where the forecourt of the Opera House now stands, on the western shore of Bennelong Point and looking right into busy Circular Quay.

The present clubhouse, at the leafy foot of Green Street and shaded by enormous Port Jackson figs, dates from the 1930s and was acquired in the early '60s.Unlike most other yacht clubs, it survives without the aid of noisy poker machines or expensive dining facilities and serves as a focal point for some of Sydney's most dedicated yachtsmen.

Not far from the Amateurs' clubhouse lives one of its most distinguished members, Australia's most celebrated maritime artist, Jack Earl. The Earl house-cum-studio, perched on the eastern edge of Kareela Avenue, has a breathtaking view down over Mosman Bay and the main harbour off to the south. Earl's boat, the delightful little double-ender, *Smokey Cape*, nods at her mooring beyond a front garden full of tropical fruit trees and hibiscus.

Up there, in a simple whitewashed studio nonetheless redolent of the rich smell of history, Earl has painted most, if not all the vessels prominent in Australia's maritime past. No other Australian marine artist, the celebrated John Allcott notwithstanding, has rendered half so many vessels with so much sensitivity, so much accuracy, so much natural feeling for the shape of ships and their peculiar motion in a seaway. Jack Earl's is a precious gift born of years before the mast. Authenticity has always been his hallmark, and for anyone who knows the sea just glancing at an Earl original arouses an instantaneous recognition.

Shell Cove, the next bay to the westward of Mosman Bay, was originally known as Hungry Bay because two convicts who escaped from Pinchgut on a raft were recaptured there, half-starved. Shell Cove takes its name from the enormous shell middens built up on its shores over thousands of years of Aboriginal occupation. The shells were crushed and burned by convict labour, extracting the lime essential to bind the mortar used in the construction of the colony's early buildings.

Around Kurraba Point lies the broad expanse of Neutral Bay, a name bestowed by Governor Phillip in 1789 when Britain and France were at war. Phillip wanted neutral shipping to continue to trade with the infant colony and therefore set aside one of the harbour's finest anchorages expressly for their use. Neutral vessels were forbidden to enter Sydney Cove or for that matter any other part of the harbour. Vessels from the colony were also forbidden to enter Neutral Bay, no doubt because Phillip feared, with good reason, that convicts would attempt to stow away on the foreign ships.

Ruth Park reminds us of the terror that bushfires struck in the hearts of the people of Sydney, and of Neutral Bay in particular, during the earliest years of settlement when so much of the North Shore was a wildwood of dense, tree-clad ridges and gullies thick with volatile undergrowth. In 1826, an enormous fire swept along the North Shore, wiping out James Milson's farmhouse and Edward Wollstonecraft's first cottage, The Crow's Nest, which gave its name to the suburb perched just beyond North Sydney.

In the 1870s another huge fire swept the North Shore from North Sydney all the way to Middle Head. This contemporary account gives some idea of the desperation it caused among the pioneer settlers: "The paddocks around the only houses in Neutral Bay made a firebreak but each residence had blankets etc. covering the dry shingle roofs . . . kept wet by passing up buckets of water. Here, along the narrow track [now Kurraba Road] snakes, opossoms, native cats, bandicoots . . . were going for their lives. Along this lucky firebreak there came, with a willing gang of helpers, Major Tunks, first Mayor of St Leonards, a fine, burly fellow of splendid physique. With an axe on his shoulder he gave his commands . . . and worked with a will until the fire had burned to the water's edge."

Neutral Bay's western shore is home to the Royal Australian Navy's aptly named submarine base, HMAS Platypus. North Sydney's office towers march along the ridge.

Neutral Bay's earliest residents were obliged to row or sail from their homes across the harbour to Sydney Cove. It was either that or walk through the bush to Lavender Bay or Milson's Point to meet the waterman, Andrews, who lived in a cottage in Careening Cove and who pulled passengers across for sixpence a head.

The North Shore Ferry Company started the first service in 1873 with the coal-fired steam paddlewheeler *Florence* plying from Circular Quay. It was from Anderson Park, overlooking the head of Neutral Bay, that Australia's intrepid aviation pioneers, Sir Charles Kingsford Smith and Sir Patrick Gordon Taylor, took off in their Lockheed Altair on July 17 1934. Kingsford Smith had had the aircraft shipped to Sydney from the United States aboard the Matson liner *Mariposa* and his original proposal was that it be landed on Circular Quay east and wheeled up the hill to Macquarie Street for a takeoff for the Melbourne centennial air race. When the authorities rejected this proposal, Smithy opted for Anderson Park and what must surely be one of the most unorthodox takeoffs in aviation history.

Gordon Taylor, Smithy's co-pilot, tells the story: "The plane was slung over the side of the ship and put on a barge. The barge was towed to Neutral Bay to the (sea) wall and the plane was wheeled ashore. In those days there were no trees there. We put the tail of the aircraft as near to the road as possible. I knew she would only just take off. We took off from the end of the park and we had nothing to spare. The wheels just left the ground as we took off."

On Neutral Bay's western shore stands the Royal Australian Navy's submarine base, HMAS Platypus. The huge black and sinister-looking subs slide in and out of the bay, contrasting vividly with the sleek white hulls of the yachts and pleasure craft moored around the corner in Careening Cove.

As its name suggests, Careening Cove, which remains one of my favourite spots in all the harbour, was originally used as a careening site for 19th century sailing vessels. The ships could easily gain access to the long, deep cove at high water and safely take the soft muddy bottom when the tide turned. At full ebb they would be left high and dry or at least sufficiently so that their crews could climb over the side and get to work.

According to fisherman and restaurateur Peter Doyle, it was in this way that mussels, which are not native Australian crustaceans, were introduced to Sydney Harbour. Mussels can still be harvested throughout the harbour. Those found below the low-water mark remain excellent eating, although those above low water are generally not fit for anything other than bait.

Careening Cove was originally known by the ghastly name of Slaughterhouse Bay. James Milson, a Lincolnshire farmer, built a cattle slaughteryard here, it is said, with timber cast up from the *Dunbar* which was wrecked with the loss of all but one survivor after her master mistook The Gap, just south of South Head, as the entrance to the harbour on a black and blustery May night in 1857.

Milson's slaughterhouse has long since gone and yet Careening Cove has retained much of its early marine character with boatsheds and sailmakers' lofts and slipways and repair yards cheek by jowl around the waterfront. On the cove's southern shore, not far from Milson Park sits the home of the Sydney Flying Squadron, Australia's oldest open boat club. Founded in 1890, the Squadron has nurtured the fantastic sail-carrying 18-footers and seen their evolution from overcanvassed and heavily-crewed cedar hulls to the incredibly skittish three-man flying machines that often do get airborne as they bounce down the harbour before a black nor'easter.

At the far eastern end of the cove, at Wudyong Point, stands the magnificent lawns and clubhouse of the Royal Sydney Yacht Squadron. Australia's oldest yacht club, the

(Right) Kirribilli's high rise is softened by the green, wooded wedge of Royal Sydney Yacht Squadron's waterfront grounds. No other yacht club in Australia and few others anywhere else enjoy such a beautiful setting.

FINNAIR
FLYING FINN
CORINTHIAN DOORS
SAILING MAGAZINE
PERFORMANCE

XEROX
XEROX

There is something universal about sunworship. A couple of devotees find themselves a quiet spot on this tiny jetty on the Kirribilli shore.

(Previous page) The ''eighteens'' are unique among Australia's racing boats in their unabashed embrace of commercialism. Festooned with corporate logos, the boats often resemble exceptionally fast floating billboards.

Squadron was founded in 1862 and today occupies one of the most glorious sites in all the harbour. At the water's edge there are haulout and hard-standing facilities for the one design racing machines like the Solings and Etchells, and the boatshed where some of the finest craftsmen on the harbour still practise the ancient boatbuilding skills. The lawns sweep up and around a pair of whitewashed whalebones and an authentic clipper's mizzen, with its cross-yard and gaff and topmast, a reminder of the grandeur of 19th century shipping.

The Squadron, easily the most imposing yacht club in Sydney, if not Australia, counts among its members some of the country's top yachtsmen. This is where Sir Frank Packer launched Australia's first America's Cup challenge in 1962. Other challenges followed in 1967 with *Dame Pattie*, in 1970 with *Gretel II*, and would-be cup defender *Steak 'n' Kidney* in 1987.

Two of Sydney's most beautiful homes dominate the hilltop overlooking Kirribilli Point. By far the bigger is Admiralty House, the Sydney home of the Governor-General. The other, right next door, is the delightful stone cottage with its high-pitched gables and scalloped, gingerbread bargeboards, known as Kirribilli House, the Sydney residence of the Prime Minister.

Surrounded by beautifully manicured lawns and carefully tended shrubs, Admiralty House stands on land granted to Robert Ryan in 1800. In 1806, Robert Campbell, the colony's most successful merchant, acquired Ryan's property. In 1842 he leased it to Lieutenant-Colonel J. G. N. Gibbes, who had a single-storey Georgian house erected there in 1843. The house had various distinguished owners including Captain George Barney, the engineer responsible for Circular Quay, Victoria Barracks at Paddington, and Fort Denison. In 1885 the house was bought by the New South Wales government as the residence for the Admirals of the British Fleet on station in Sydney. Twelve British Admirals resided there until 1913 when the house was lent to the Federal Government for use as the Sydney residence for the Governor-General. Admiralty House finally became Commonwealth property by Crown grant in 1948.

Kirribilli House dates from the mid-1850s but it really owes its existence to the indefatigable Prime Minister, William Morris Hughes. Following a public outcry he approved its compulsory purchase in 1920 and headed off the property's subdivision and sale to private developers. In 1956 the Federal Government finally got around to refurbishing the six-room, two-storey cottage as a residence for official guests and as the PM's home in Sydney, away from The Lodge in Canberra.

Milson's Point, that shadowed nub of land beneath the Harbour Bridge's northern pylon, was once part of a 20-hectare estate granted to James Milson, a 23-year-old free settler and farmer when he settled there in 1806. Very close to the present site of the north-eastern pylon, Milson built a slab cottage with a shingle roof, sandstone-flagged floors and whitewashed walls. It was built, Milson said, "on a raft of seashells, white as cheese, left there by Johnny Blackfellow through a thousand years".

Besides growing fruit, cereals and vegetables, the industrious Milson ran a dairy herd and sold the milk to visiting ships' crews. Milson's milk became so popular that his cottage soon became known as The Milk House. But farming on such hard and stony land proved less than profitable and soon Milson turned to selling sandstone ballast to the masters of sailing ships who, having discharged their cargoes from Europe, found little in the young colony worth taking home to the Old World. Milson quarried the sandstone blocks from his own hillsides and lightered it in a punt to vessels at anchor in the stream or alongside berths at Circular Quay. Milson's punt across the harbour became a forerunner of the steam-powered horse ferry that ran from Milson's Point to Dawes Point on the opposite southern shore and indeed of the great bridge that now arcs directly above the route he once plied.

Legal &
General

Seen through a telephoto lens from the rooftops of Walsh Bay, Luna Park and Lavender Bay loom much closer than in reality. Just west of the bridge, Walsh Bay is one of the busiest parts of the harbour.

(Previous page) Lavender Bay takes on the appearance of Byron's wine-dark sea as rain clouds sweep across Milson's Point. Much of Luna Park is now demolished.

James Milson's indefatigable industry was to be rewarded by the kind of bureaucratic arrogance and indifference that even today, nearly two centuries later, arouses a good deal of bitterness and resentment. Milson lost the title deeds to his land during the catastrophic bushfire that razed virtually the entire north shore in November 1825. Accounts say "the heat and hot wind excelled all that we had ever experienced in the Colony. It was, in some parts of the town, 104 degrees . . . Sydney was more like the mouth of Vesuvius than anything else. An extensive and frightful conflagration occurred in the woods . . ."

Milson, who was absent during the fire, returned to find his home destroyed, his family having barely escaped with their lives. The iron box in which he kept the deeds to his land was melted beyond recognition. Although he made repeated applications for copies of the papers, the colonial bureaucrats refused him time and again. For some unexplained reason, the man whose industry had contributed so much to the prosperity of the settlement was treated as a squatter and finally evicted from the land he had owned and worked for more than 20 years. Tough and white-bearded Milson survived to be 90 and despite the misfortunes he became one of Sydney's leading citizens and a prominent yachtsman.

Blue's Point, the crescent-shaped neck opposite McMahon's Point and immediately to the west of Milson's Point, was named for the harbour's first waterman, Billy Blue. A West Indian seaman, he became known as the "Old Commodore". Blue was one of the earliest Water Bailiffs (Water Police Superintendent) and as such enjoyed spectacular harbour views from an extraordinary octagonal house built for him on Bennelong Point. When he left the government service in 1817, Blue was rewarded with a grant of 32 hectares on the point that still bears his name. Here he grew fruit and vegetables and carried them across the harbour to Jack the Miller's Point, where he sold them. When a track was cleared through the bush linking Blue's Point with the farms on the North Shore, Blue charged for ferrying passengers and goods to and from what became known as Miller's Point.

Sydney's North Shore was settled much later than the southern side. As Ruth Park so eloquently reminds us, it was a long time before the Shore flew flags of smoke from chimney fires. "The first pictures," she says, "show these deep sheltered coves crowned with small, yellow beaches, all-year-round creeks splitting the green slopes above like white veins. Waterfalls are everywhere, rushing down the sandstone cliffs, for this was a well-watered land, and indeed, even today from the air the whole terrain is marked with the sculptured forms of creek beds, drained lagoons and old ponds."

Between McMahon's Point and Milson's Point lies Lavender Bay. It was named for George Lavender, boatswain on the convict hulk *Phoenix* which housed prisoners awaiting transportation to Norfolk Island, the dreaded Devil's Island of the Pacific. The 600-ton *Phoenix* very nearly came to grief on the Sow and Pigs reef, the treacherous rocky outcrop just inside South Head, when inward bound from London on August 10 1824. She struck the reef but did not sink. She was hauled off, but condemned as unseaworthy.

The colonial authorities nevertheless decided to make good use of her as a convict halfway house and she was taken to a berth on Goat Island's western shore. Here, colonially reconvicted prisoners were housed while they worked on the island in chain gangs, chipping away at the magnificent sandstone, reputed to be of the finest quality. In 1831, after Surveyor-General Major Thomas Mitchell warned that the island was in danger of being quarried away, the *Phoenix* and her convicts were taken across to a berth in Lavender Bay.

There, men were often shackled in irons for months at a time while they waited for ships bound for Norfolk Island. In 1833, Governor Bourke moved the prisoners out of their unhealthy quarters aboard the hulk and sent them ashore into huts on Goat Island.

George Lavender married Billy Blue's daughter, Susannah, and in 1834 followed his father-in-law's example and became a waterman, ferrying passengers, farm produce and livestock from his property across the harbour and back again.

Middle Harbour

In 1788, Governor Phillip described Port Jackson as "the bay of a hundred Coves". Today's charts of the Main Harbour show 56 bays, 10 coves, two creeks and two rivers, the Parramatta and the Lane Cove. In Middle Harbour there are nine bays, two coves and one creek. In North Harbour, one bay and three coves. That makes a grand total of 66 bays and 15 coves, although many of the so-called bays (a bay is described in the *Oxford Companion to Ships and the Sea* simply as "an indentation in the coastline between two headlands") are really parts of larger bays. There are, as P. R. "Inky" Stephensen points out in his *History and Description of Sydney Harbour*, "coves within bays and bays within coves". All in all, an impressive body of water.

And indeed the harbour itself is so vast that it has been divided into three distinct arms which are large and sufficiently separate to be properly regarded as harbours in their own right. Each branch of the harbour has its own staunch supporters when it comes to arguing about which is the most beautiful. Those who have the good fortune to live on or near Middle Harbour swear that their bush-clad bailiwick is the be-all and end-all of harbours. They may well be right.

Much of Middle Harbour remains pretty much as it was in April 1788 when Governor Phillip and a small party of Marines hacked their way through the bush, right to the head of Middle Harbour. Their journey marked the first European land exploration of the Harbour's North Shore. Phillip may have been awed by the raw natural beauty of the place but at the same time he was clearly less than impressed with its agricultural potential. A farmer as well as a seaman, he knew exactly what to look for when it came to arable land and there was precious little of it on those wild sandstone bluffs. Phillip's views of Middle Harbour were confirmed by succeeding generations of settlers who regarded Middle Harbour as a fine place in which to picnic, but in those far-off days they would never have dreamed of living permanently so far from the centre of things at Sydney Cove.

Apparently lit from within by some magical lantern, twisted angophoras, like this one at Middle Harbour, stood with their roots wedded to rock and salt water when the first European settlers came to Sydney.

(Right) At the base of mighty Dobroyd Head, a steep wave suddenly rises up to become a plume of foam dashed upon the rocks. This is the Dobroyd bombora, the graveyard of many a ship and many a mariner.

(Previous page) Clontarf's clear water and golden sand belie the notion that Sydney Harbour is polluted. In fact, not since the coming of the Europeans, has the harbour been so clean.

The great brooding bulk of saltsea-blasted Dobroyd Head stands like an implacable guard at the entrance to Middle Harbour. One of the focal points of the magnificent Sydney Harbour National Park, Dobroyd's great bulk, unsullied by any European structure (save for the tiny doll's house of a light at Grotto Point), serves as a glorious, permanent reminder of the way all the harbour once looked not so many years ago. There is a timeless, spiritual quality about that great shaggy stone head with its thin thatch of grey-green gorse up top and its frothy white beard on the shelving rocks below.

Here, if one looks closely and uses a little imagination, one can see the incised footprints of the Aboriginals' ancestors. Carved in the ancient grey stone and now weathered smooth after thousands of years, they show the way to what is believed to have been a sacred Aboriginal corroboree ground — a site where elaborate rituals and initiations were performed by the much-feared Camaraigal warriors who ruled the harbour's northern shore from Lane Cove to Middle Harbour and who have given their name to the suburb of Cammeray. Here, in the caves not far from the water's edge, are Aboriginal hand stencils and carvings of fish and whales.

In his excellent and deeply moving account of the destruction of the Sydney tribes, *When The Sky Fell Down*, Keith Willey tells us that here, and indeed throughout the Sydney Harbour area, the various Aboriginal clan groups lived to an ordered pattern. They were generally at peace with each other and in complete harmony with the natural rhythms of the bush, where the spirits of their ancestors dwelt in every rock and tree and waterhole.

"At regular intervals, the old men would declare a time of initiation", he writes. For days the warriors would dance on the bora grounds while 'carrahdys', witchdoctors, whirled the sacred bullroarers. Women in their far camps, hearing the sound, would stir uneasily and huddle closer about their fires, for knowledge of such matters was forbidden."

Below the cliff face at Dobroyd Head lies perhaps the most dangerous stretch of water in all the harbour. Known simply as the Bombora, it consists of a large, barely submerged rock shelf where, as Ruth Park writes, "the water glides greasily in a tilting circle". The Bombora has claimed dozens of lives over the years. The first was Commander John Gowland and his boatswain, who were drowned there on August 11 1874 when their survey boat was caught in the sudden, powerful surge and dashed onto the rocks.

Dobroyd Head has several excellent walking tracks that skirt the cliff tops and provide one of the most spectacular views of the harbour. The walks are linked with Dobroyd Scenic Drive, an oval-shaped road that encircles Tania Park at the very top of the bushland reserve. Below the drive and almost hidden in Crater Valley are the remains of seven driftwood and stone huts thrown up by squatters and fishermen who were meant to have been ejected when the area was incorporated into the Sydney Harbour National Park. The huts first appeared in the 1920s and during the Depression years they became permanent homes for families who had been evicted from their own homes and were forced to live off the land or, more accurately, off the sea.

Grotto Point, first dedicated as a recreation reserve in 1912, is now part of Sydney Harbour National Park. It has the distinction of being one of the first landforms in the harbour named by Europeans. The name was bestowed in January 1788 by the boat crew which Governor Phillip sent to examine Middle Harbour before his decision to move the First Fleet north from Botany Bay. The name is derived from the caves in which they found the Camaraigal people living as they had been for tens of thousands of years.

The delicate little Grotto Point light, one of the most beautiful in the harbour, is also one of its smallest. Surrounded now by a white picket fence, its delightful whitewashed tower and delicate domed roof always remind me of Aegean lighthouses. Although it contrasts sharply with the stunted salt-blasted bush and rock around it, at the same time it fits in snugly and seems to exude an air of eternity appropriate to its role.

North-west of Grotto Point and opposite The Spit is Clontarf, once an ancient Aboriginal corroboree ground and now named for the Victorian pleasure resort on Dublin Bay. It was here on March 12 1868 that the 23-year-old Prince Alfred, the Duke of

(Left) Like some fantastic oyster shell, this stone cliff face, scoured and scarred by aeons of weathering, sits at the very tip of Grotto Point at the entrance to Middle Harbour.

(Overleaf) Middle Harbour's Castle Rock Beach is lapped by cool, clear water. Scores of beaches like this remain part of the national estate, protected and maintained in pristine condition but at the same time free to all.

(Above) Generations of Sydney-siders have learned to swim at Clontarf's saltwater pool. Enclosed by sharkproof netting, the baths are a favourite place for parents to tutor their children in the art of dogpaddle.

(Left) The Spit Bridge, the bane of motorists when its roadway yawns opens to allow the tall masts of yachts to pass between Middle Harbour and the main harbour, also is one of the northern beaches' main arteries.

(Overleaf) No other city in the world can boast the kind of sublime harbour views that residents of Sydney — and Middle Harbour in particular — take for granted.

Edinburgh, was shot by a Liverpool Irishman, Henry O'Farrell, an anti-royalist Fenian. The prince survived but O'Farrell did not. Seized before he could fire a second shot, he was hanged just over a month later at Sydney's Darlinghurst Gaol.

Today, Clontarf exudes a lazy informality. Its homes, set back from a clean, golden beach, are invariably large and for the most part, luxurious. As a child I journeyed down here in our family boats for barbecue picnics not unlike the one the young prince was supposed to be enjoying on that fateful day. People still come from all over Sydney for exactly the same good reasons and in high summer, Clontarf, like so many of the lovely harbourside parks, often has a distinctly Mediterranean air with large immigrant families spread out on the lawns and the beach.

It was in a superb waterfront studio-cum-boatshed at Sandy Bay, just next to Clontarf, that Australia's greatest yacht designer, Ben Lexcen, worked to perfect many of the yachts that made him famous throughout the world. Ben Lexcen died tragically at the age of 53 in 1988 but left behind a legacy of intelligent good humour as well as a towering reputation for producing some of the world's fastest sailboats, including the historic 1983 America's Cup winner, *Australia II*. Lexcen and his wife, Yvonne, shared a magnificent home high above Middle Harbour's Powder Hulk Bay. Here, the man respected as a gentle genius, fed his tame kookaburras and tinkered with the design concepts that set him apart as a refreshing, original thinker in one of the sailing world's toughest fields.

The Spit, directly opposite Clontarf, also has extensive picnic areas and beaches, although here things tend to be a lot more crowded with a jumble of car parks, chandlers, boatsheds and marinas. The views from water level are certainly spectacular, but to appreciate truly The Spit it is necessary to go aloft, either on Spit Road that twists and turns and leads back up the hill toward Spit Junction or, on the other side, up the old white-painted Gallipoli Steps that plod up the rocky hillside to the Esplanade at Seaforth. Ruth Park says it all from her poet's eye view: "The unwinding view is a wonderful one, especially at sunset when The Spit's myriad little boats are painted pink and the polished water of Pearl Bay reflects dazzling windows from Beauty Point to Seaforth Bluff."

She recalls that for many years bullock teams were ferried over the narrow channel on punts. "Ponderous in weight and strength were those ox wagons, built like ships to withstand all the forces of nature and of time.They brought to Sydney timber, produce, fodder and lime from the shellbanks of Pittwater." The present bridge, a functional if unlovely structure with a drawbridge rising vertically to allow for the passage of yachts, replaced the rickety old wooden structure which replaced the punts and stood until 1958.

The Pearl Bay and Beauty Point areas were not developed until the mid to late 1930s but even then and as astonishing as it seems today, not a single bid was offered when the waterfront land was first offered to the public. In the late '30s, waterfront blocks went for as little as £400. Today some are near the million dollar mark.

South of Beauty Point is the aptly named Long Bay which stretches right back down into Cammeray and embraces a number of picturesquely named bays and coves incuding Quaker's Hat Bay (named for its shape), Saltpan Creek and Willoughby Bay.Without exception, Middle Harbour's bays and coves are magnificent with almost all the foreshore land bush-clad and much of it dedicated as public recreational reserve.

Middle Harbour's northern arteries which stretch all the way up past the Roseville Bridge to the bushland of the Davidson Park State Recreation Area in Ku-ring-gai and Warringah, share the same glorious heritage of grey-green trees fringing the sandstone shores.

Off to the west are the twin arms of Sugarloaf Bay, named in the 19th century for the distinctive high, cone shape of the inlet's middle cape, known as Middle Cove. The hill, in what is now the Harold Reid Reserve and known simply as the Sugarloaf, was first seen by Europeans during Phillip's exploration of Middle Harbour in April 1788.

South of Sugarloaf Bay's south arm is Castlecrag, the area which gets its name from the huge rocky outcrop there, marked on the earliest charts as Edinburgh Castle. Castlecrag is known best for its many superb homes and their beautiful views down through the bushland to the harbour. Here is an entire suburb which owes its existence to the design genius of American architect Walter Burley Griffin, the man who in 1912 won an international competition and laid out the national capital. Burley Griffin, a colleague of the much more famous American architect, Frank Lloyd Wright, not only designed Castlecrag's twisting streets, he also named them for the various parts of a medieval castle — The Battlement, The Scarp, The Tor Walk, The Barbette, The Parapet, The Rampart and so on. Burley Griffin and his wife, Marion, lived in Castlecrag (Number 8, The Parapet) for 12 years before his death in India in 1937.

Below Castlecrag and across the lovely, sheltered waters of Sailor's Bay lies Northbridge, the suburb that takes its name from the extraordinary Gothic style suspension bridge which once spanned the Middle Harbour Gorge. Although the superb sandstone arches remain, the old suspension bridge was condemned as unsafe in 1936 and subsequently replaced by a concrete structure. The original bridge, constructed in 1891, was regarded as the engineering marvel of its time. It was part of an elaborate land development programme in which promoters hoped to take steam tram transportation to their real estate properties. The developers were, however, unable to pay for the bridge, and its contractors were forced to charge tolls to recover their costs. The State Government eventually took over the bridge and paid for the upgrading work.

Above Sugarloaf Bay and around Yeoland Point is the long northerly stretch of Bantry Bay. Not at all like the original Bantry Bay in Ireland it is, nevertheless, like its namesake, a place of deep spiritual significance. The tranquil bay is enclosed on its three sides by the rugged beauty of the bushland within Davidson Park, an area set aside as a public reserve in 1923. The Camaraigal people, who fished around the bay's foreshores from their rough bark canoes, made good use of the flat sandstone rock near the water's edge for their carvings connecting the spiritual world of their Dreaming with their everyday lives as hunters and gatherers. Here, almost 80 rock carvings — the most extensive in the Sydney region and a collection which some archaeologists believe to be the finest group of its kind in the world — include beautifully wrought fish, wallabies, a dingo, shields, a bark canoe, baskets, bags, boomerangs, circles, stone axes, snakes, an echidna and an exceptionally detailed whale. One carving shows two men, one carrying a bark canoe. In 1917, Bantry Bay became a banned area when the Department of Mines took it over as an explosive storage depot. By the 1970s, when the Mines Department relinquished the depot and moved out, environmentalists seized on the area as an outstanding example of harbourside bushland in original condition. We are all enriched by its continued preservation.

The steep, wooded shores of Middle Harbour's Sailor's Bay offer security from virtually all weathers. Many of the finest harbourside homes here command expensive price tags.

South of The Spit and on its eastern shore lies Shell Cove and the lovely little Chinaman's Beach. The site of a 19th century Chinese market garden (Ah Sue's, according to Sands's *NSW Directory of 1890*), the area immediately behind the beach now forms the beautifully maintained Rosherville Reserve. Past Wy-ar-gine Point

Cradled in Middle Harbour's southern arm lie some of the most idyllic homes in Sydney. This is one of the earliest. Situated on the water's edge, it commands a magnificent outlook to unspoiled bushland and crystal-clear water.

(Overleaf) Middle Harbour's northern arm is blessed in that much of it remains exactly the way it was when the Europeans arrived. Save for the pleasure cruiser, this is a view one imagines the Aborigines must have shared long ago.

and cradled in Middle Harbour's southern arm, all the way down to the lee of Middle Head is Hunter's Bay, named for John Hunter, Captain of the *Sirius* and the second Governor of New South Wales. Unfortunately, people today tend to refer to the bay simply as Balmoral which is in fact the name of the suburb that borders the bay.

Balmoral is named for the British royal family's Scottish estate at Braemar in Aberdeenshire and is one of the most delightful beaches in all the harbour. In fact there are two lovely beaches here, separated by Rocky Point, a marvellous bushy little nub that offers a special kind of tranquillity for anyone prepared to sit on its well-worn rocks and scan the Tasman horizon out through the Heads.

The northernmost beach is Edwards Beach, named for the old whaling captain who retired to a 10-hectare property there about the middle of the 19th century and who was the first to sight the wreckage of the *Dunbar* in 1857. During the 1870s and 1880s, the scrub behind Edwards Beach was dotted with the huts and camp sites of an odd assortment of loners and drifters who generally kept to themselves. It was also the site of another of the famous harbourside artists' camps. Julian Ashton lived there with Arthur Streeton and Livingstone Hopkins, *The Bulletin* cartoonist, known as Hop.

Balmoral Beach, which is about twice the size of Edwards Beach, lies just south of Rocky Point and sweeps right around to the naval base HMAS Penguin, with its hospital and underwater medicine centre. Just to the east of the Royal Australian Navy base is the tiny sliver of golden sand known as Cobbler's Beach, which must be one of the smallest and most delightful of the harbour's beaches. Cobbler's sits snug within Middle Head, which is part of the Sydney Harbour National Park.

Although much of inner Middle Head is Department of Defence property and therefore off-limits, the public does have access to virtually the entire headland and indeed all the waterfront property that stretches right around into the Main Harbour to George's Head, where a military reserve once again breaks the National Park land at Chowder Bay. Between Middle Head and George's Head lies Obelisk Bay, a tiny fingernail of a beach named for the slender whitewashed obelisk that serves as a turning marker for inbound vessels. Obelisk Bay is an excellent anchorage in a hard nor'easter and despite its size one of the most popular spots for the harbour's cruising sailors.

Off Balmoral wharf they may catch nothing more exciting than yellowtail or leather-jacket, but that's beside the point. Fishing is its own reward.

(Left) Chinaman's Beach maintains its pristine purity. This is the way it was before Europeans came.

George's Head, named for King George III (the monarch who lost Britain's American colonies and in the process gave impetus to Australia's founding), was throughout the 19th and much of the 20th century regarded as being of particular strategic importance to the defence of Sydney. In 1871 the enormous sum of £210 000 was spent pushing Military Road and Bradley's Head Road through the bush so that a battery of heavy guns could be installed on the headland commanding the harbour entrance.

According to one contemporary account: "The guns were built up with wood so that they assumed equal diameters at each end. After three months of incessant labour by 250 soldiers, during which about one-third were incapacitated by accident, the guns arrived at their destination and

Amateur and professional painters alike are drawn to Balmoral's beauty.

(Previous page) Balmoral. A far cry indeed from the Scottish landscape for which it was named. The beach, facing Middle Harbour's mouth and beyond it the open sea, is one of the most beautiful in Sydney.

(Right) On Wy-ar-gine Point, sandstone ledges shelve gently down toward the harbour sparkling in the early morning light. Beyond North Head lies the sea.

were placed in position. Such a crop of broken and twisted limbs, sprains and severe flesh wounds were seldom, if ever known before.''

The Army still moves its artillery pieces around and about George's Head but these days the operation involves the much less arduous and much more spectacular business of slinging the field guns under huge Chinook helicopters and whisking them away.

George's Head also is believed to have been the site of an unsuccessful attempt by Governor Lachlan Macquarie to establish some sort of Aboriginal village with European-style huts and gardens. It was known as Bungaree's Farm after ''King Bungaree'', an Aboriginal who took to wearing a British military uniform and a brass gorget around his neck inscribed with his coat of arms featuring a kangaroo and an emu. One of Macquarie's last acts of governorship was to introduce the 16 Aboriginal families living there to his successor, Sir Thomas Brisbane. The village fell to ruin when the Aboriginal people returned to their traditional lifestyles, fishing, hunting and gathering and living in the caves and shelving rocks that marked the cliff above the harbour.

Taylor's Bay is the last of the harbour's major indentations before Bradley's Head. Another excellent anchorage in a nor'easterly blow, the bay, with its tiny beach, its foreshores covered by shallow sandstone ledges and above them the pink flesh of the angophoras, has always struck me as being very much representative of the way the harbour always was. This, however, is no longer strictly true. Peter Doyle, who lives in Watson's Bay, points out that the eucalypts that once grew right along the outstretched western arm of Taylor's Bay to Bradley's Head and placed an impenetrable green screen in front of the city skyline, now are so severely thinned by airborne detergents and chemicals used in sewage treatment, that he can now clearly see the city buildings from his front verandah. The entire peninsula is under the control of National Parks and Wildlife authorities who administer the Sydney Harbour National Park. When I brought this to their attention, moves were immediately made to investigate the possibility of regenerating the bush plants and eucalypts. It is a project which may well extend to other National Park sites throughout the harbour.

304
53

The Central Harbour

NO OTHER PART OF THE HARBOUR foreshores has so many fine old homes, or for that matter, so many unspeakable high-rise apartment towers, as Darling Point. The point, originally named Mrs Darling's Point in honour of Governor Ralph Darling's wife, Elizabeth, is on a par with Vaucluse in terms of real estate prices and notions of residential exclusivity. Originally known as ''Yara-nabe'' and dominated by a steep, rocky and heavily-wooded ridge, Darling Point was effectively cut off from the settlement at Sydney Cove by a broad swamp and creek at what is now Rushcutters Bay. But in the early 1830s, Daniel (later Sir Daniel) Cooper, one of the colony's wealthiest landholders, pushed what is now New South Head Road out to his properties around Watson's Bay. A bridge thrown over the Rushcutters Bay swamp allowed timber-getters to strip the magnificent stands of tall red cedar that grew from the gullies along the ridge. So savage were they in stripping away the bush that erosion soon washed off the rocks what little topsoil there was, and threatened to destroy the entire area.

The man who saved Darling Point, Major Thomas Livingstone Mitchell, soldier, explorer, linguist, and author, was to become one of its most distinguished early residents. The point was almost bare, with white sand everywhere on all sides when Mitchell, in a letter to the Colonial Secretary, suggested that ''these gentry [the timber-getters] should be shut out from Mrs Darling's Ridge''.

Mitchell, who was Surveyor-General of New South Wales from 1828 until his death in 1855, needed an exceptionally large house. He and his wife had 12 children who were all reared in Carthona (a Spanish word meaning the meeting of the waters), the magnificent Lake Windemere-style mansion he built there and which remains one of Sydney's finest and most beautifully preserved colonial homes. Mitchell, who among his many other attributes was a talented amateur mason, carved much of the ornamental stonework, including many of the keystones for the window arches and the main door.

Before he came to Sydney, Mitchell surveyed the battlefields for the Peninsula War and is credited with working out Wellington's lines of defence. In Australia, ''this crusty and quarrelsome Scottish Tory'' became a distinguished explorer, trekking off to the Murray, the Murrumbidgee and the Darling, and as far as the beautiful open grazing and agricultural country between the Murray and the Victorian coast west of Port Phillip, the country he called ''Australia Felix''.

Although there seems to be no direct historical reference or proof for it, Mitchell may well have been responsible for conferring the entirely appropriate Latin name, Felix (happy, fortunate, prosperous), on the bay between Point Piper and Woollahra Point which contains Lady Martin Beach. In his history of Woollahra, Vince Kelly tells how Mitchell, returning to Carthona in an open carriage after dining at Victoria Barracks, was attacked by muggers (known then as footpads) who robbed

Garden Island is much more than a naval dockyard. It is a living museum. Among the splendid colonial architecture are these two fine buildings, the Sail Loft and Rigging Shed (circa 1887) and the Tarakan Building with its double-decker verandahs, named for HMAS *Tarakan*, a tank landing ship which exploded and killed nine seamen in the 1950s.

(Left) St Marks, Darling Point. The simple elegance of its Gothic-style tower and crypt represents the finest work of the convict architect, Edmund Blacket, who was known as "Australia's Christopher Wren".

(Pages 130–131) War and Peace Australian style. Bathers pay homage to the Sun God at Woolloomooloo Baths while across the bay, missile-carrying frigates and tankers rest easy at Garden Island's Naval Dockyard.

Elizabeth Bay from Darling Point.

(Overleaf) Rushcutters Bay is home to the Cruising Yacht Club of Australia. It is from here each Boxing Day that the bulk of the Sydney–Hobart Race fleet sets sail.

him of his boots, cash and watch and chain. As a result, Mitchell is said to have built a stone cottage on what is now Yarranabbe Road for the use of the police who, until then, simply clanked about on horseback and whose numbers were supplemented by watchmen.

Among the other elegant and historic buildings in Darling Point is refrigeration pioneer Thomas Sutcliffe Mort's mansion in Greenoaks Avenue. Built in 1874 and originally named Greenoaks, it was subsequently renamed Bishopscourt, and is now the residence of the Anglican Archbishop of Sydney.

There also, on the corner of Greenoaks Avenue and Darling Point Road, is arguably the most beautiful little church in Sydney. St Mark's was designed by the very young Edmund Blacket and may well have been his first commission in Australia. Its foundation stone was laid in 1848 and although the gold rushes of the 1850s all but stopped its construction when labourers, masons and everyone else it seems, went off to seek their fortune in the diggings, St Mark's eventually rose to become a Sydney landmark, standing on the highest part of the ridge with its stone belltower looking down on the harbour like a sentinel. It was described in the 1870s as "a perfect toy of a church, (which) sits as plumply on its stone mound as a castle, done in white sugar, on a twelfth night cake".

Although it has been suggested that the infamous rush-cutter murders in 1788 took place in Cockle Bay (now Darling Harbour), it is generally accepted that the two dead convicts, William Okey and Samuel Davis, were in fact speared to death in the long deep bay between Darling Point and Elizabeth Bay–Garden Island, which is now known as Rushcutters Bay. The bay, at the beginning of European occupation, was an estuary for two freshwater streams. Fringed by swampy foreshores lined with mangroves, the bay was choked with rushes which were much sought after for thatching. Okey and Davis were the first Europeans to be killed by Aboriginals. A Marines officer named Campbell took them down to the bay by boat and left them there with a tent. Their orders were to cut rushes, but according to the official inquiry they were seen to have taken an Aboriginal canoe drawn up near a traditional fishing ground and to have therefore provoked the attack.

Bradley reports that when Captain Campbell returned, "he found the tent but not the Men, finding some blood near the Tent he followed it to the Mangrove bushes where they found both men dead and lying at some distance from each other. One of them (Okey) had three spears in him and one side of his head beat in. The other Man had no apparent wound but a blow on the forehead." Surgeon John White concluded that Davis, a youth, had "only some trifling marks of violence about him and may have died of fright".

The rush-cutters' tools, which included hatchets and billhooks, were missing and presumed stolen, but Governor Phillip placed the blame on provocation by the convicts. "In this case it is clearly proved that the first injury had been offered by the unfortunate men who paid so dearly for their dishonesty and disobedience of orders," he reported. Bradley believed the murders were a form of pay-back for an earlier incident in which "a Convict had killed one of the Natives some days before by cutting him across the belly with his knife. They have attack'd our people when they have met them unarmed, but that did not happen until after they had been very ill treated by us in the lower part of the Harbour and fired upon at Botany Bay by the French."

The humane and gentle Governor Phillip was a man who had the greatest respect for the Aboriginals. The very next day he and an armed party of 12 set out to find the murderers, not to punish them but to try to prevent further bloodshed. Phillip and his men marched 51 gruelling kilometres through the bush to the shores of Botany Bay where they camped on the beach. The next day, as Keith Willey observes in *When The Sky Fell Down*, "one of those curious incidents occurred which emphasise how much of what happened between white and black in those earliest years remains unexplained".

Here is Phillip's account: ". . . the next morning, tho' fifty canoes were drawn up on the beach, we could not find a single person; but on our return, keeping for some time near the sea-coast, we came to a cove where a number of the natives were assembled, I believe more than what belonged to that particular spot. Though we were within ten yards when we first discovered each other, I had barely time to order the party to halt before numbers appeared in arms, and the foremost of them, as he advanced, made signs for us to retire, but upon my going up to him, making signs of friendship, he gave his spear to another and in less than three minutes we were surrounded by two hundred and twelve men, numbers of women and children were at a small distance, and whether by their superiority of numbers, for we were only twelve, or from their not being accustomed to act with treachery, the moment the friendship I offered was accepted on their side they joined us, most of them laying down their spears and stone hatchets with the greatest confidence, and afterwards brought down some of their women to receive the little articles we had given them."

Phillip found none of the rush-cutters' belongings or any other evidence to link the gathering with the dead men. "We parted on friendly terms and I was more than ever convinced of the necessity of placing a confidence in these people as the only means of avoiding a dispute," he wrote.

Just 40 years later, most of the Aboriginals had gone and the land given over to the cultivation of tobacco, corn, vegetables and fruit. In the 1870s the marshlands, sandbanks and mangroves which were once the home to an army of mudcrabs and fish, were filled in and reclaimed, like so many similar spots all around the harbour, for recreational purposes. Today, the lush green lawns of Rushcutters Bay Park show how extensive the old bay was. Rushcutters Bay is the home of the Cruising Yacht Club of Australia, the club which, despite its name, is concerned almost exclusively with ocean racing. It is doubtful whether any other part of the harbour contains as many boats. The bay, especially with the approach of Boxing Day and the start of the annual Sydney–Hobart Yacht Race, is crammed with hundreds of boats. It is a scene repeated to a lesser extent in Elizabeth Bay, the next bay to the westward.

Elizabeth Bay was named by Governor Macquarie in honour of his wife and today the name is applied not only to the waters and foreshores but also to the densely populated residential area whose high-rise apartment towers march up the steeply sloping ridges that run back toward King's Cross. Few other parts of the harbour command more extensive views than those in Elizabeth Bay. The homes, most of them blessed with an easterly aspect, look eight kilometres down the harbour with uninterrupted views past the Mosman shore and Bradley's Head to North Head.

Standing as a solitary reminder of the grandeur of the colonial past in Elizabeth Bay is the house which John Verge designed in 1838 for the explorer, naturalist, Colonial Secretary and first Speaker of the Legislative Council, Alexander Macleay.

Above Elizabeth Bay is the long, grey arm of the Garden Island Dockyard, Sydney headquarters of the Royal Australian Navy. Although it is joined now to the mainland and generally off-limits to the public, Garden Island remains a fascinating repository of Australia's colonial and maritime history. Originally 600 metres long and 200 metres wide, it lay along a south to north axis and was separated from the mainland by a 33-metre channel off Point Piper.

In 1788, the island was set aside as a vegetable garden for the ship's company aboard HMS *Sirius* and in the first 40 years of settlement it was transferred from ship to ship serving the same purpose. The Sirius garden was situated in the fertile saddle formed between the island's distinctive twin humps. The first crops raised in the colony, onions and corn, were harvested here.

From its bloody beginnings as the site of one of the colony's earliest murders in which two convicts were speared to death by blacks, Rushcutters Bay has become the harbour's finest yacht basin.

Bustling up Woolloomooloo Bay, a pilot boat as squat and unlovely as she is functional and seaworthy, makes her way to her berth at the head of the bay.

(Right) Woolloomooloo terraces. The old waterfront district, long the haunt of sailors and labourers, is rapidly being taken over by young, middle-class professionals.

(Overleaf) Ratings aboard the guided missile destroyer, HMAS *Brisbane*, stand by with their pipes poised ready to convert the bosun's orders into shrill signals passed down from Nelson's navy.

The island was dedicated for strictly naval purposes in 1866. The Sail Loft and Rigging Shed, both still in use, date from this time and remain the oldest buildings on the island. Across the lawn from the path leading up from the wharf roadway is a rock inscribed with the initials FM and the date 1788. Although no one, not even meticulous Garden Island historian Lou Lind, can be certain, the initials are generally believed to be those of Frederick Meredith, a seaman aboard HMS *Sirius*. Meredith may well have been among the party sent to the island in February 1788 to establish the original garden. If this were true, the initials would be the oldest extant European markings in Australia.

One of the most interesting buildings on the island is the Boatshed, a delightful weatherboard structure, prefabricated in England and erected on the island in the 1880s. Garden Island was acquired by the Royal Australian Navy in July 1913 when it was used for the repair and maintenance of the Australian Squadron.

Although in 1856 the NSW Government gave the British Admiralty the use of the island, in 1923 — 12 years after the Royal Australian Navy came into being — the State government sought to cancel the agreement and regain control of the island. After a long court battle, the High Court ruled in the State's favour. The Commonwealth resumed the island under wartime powers and at the war's end in 1945 spent £638,000 on its purchase.

In 1940, Sir Alexander Gibb ended a study of 16 possible sites across the nation with a recommendation to the Commonwealth Government that an enormous graving dock be built at the southern end of Garden Island. Work on what became known as the Captain Cook Graving Dock, 347 metres long, 45 metres wide and 14 metres deep, started in May 1940. By the time it was completed in March 1945 it was capable of servicing the biggest aircraft carriers and battleships in the world. Towering over it all is the giant "hammer-head" crane. One of the biggest in the world, it is capable of lifting 250 tonnes.

In the earliest days of settlement, Woolloomooloo Bay, the long bay behind Garden Island and just to the west, was known as Garden Cove. Together with Sydney Cove and Farm Cove, it was one of the three principal anchorages for ships in the harbour, despite being only 250 metres long, barely 400 metres wide at its entrance and narrowing to scarcely 250 metres at its base.

In 1793, Major Francis Grose, the acting administrator left to run the colony on Phillip's departure, made a grant of 40 hectares in what was known as the Vale of Woolloomooloo to John Palmer, the colony's Commissary General (the keeper of the Government Stores) and who had been purser aboard the *Sirius*. Palmer, a steady, industrious man, soon branched out as a flour miller, ship owner, Bass Strait sealer and rural land holder. He used the Aboriginal name, ''Woolloomooloo'', to name his estate and at the head of the Garden Cove built what was reported to be one of the finest houses in the colony. In the 1790s, Aboriginals and Europeans mixed at Woolloomooloo in the colony's first organised sporting contests. These involved demonstrations of Aboriginal skills in spear-throwing and spear-dodging, and warriors from distant clans came like Knights Errant to show their skills and to see first-hand the strange white men of whom they had heard extraordinary reports.

Woolloomooloo Bay, as it soon became known, boasted several major boatbuilding yards and as early as February 1804 an official list of schooners and sloops belonging to individuals in the colony showed that several were Woolloomooloo-built. Dan Sheehy was one of the most prominent early builders. It was Sheehy who gave form to the radical lines of *The Australian*, the so-called ''mackerel boat'' designed by Richard Harnett.

Charles Cowper, NSW Premier and member for East Sydney (which included Woolloomooloo), had the mudflats at the head of the bay dredged and built over by a semi-circular wharf which was soon extended around the eastern shore to accommodate the colliers owned by coal baron John Brown and smacks that supplied the fish markets.

During the gold rush of the 1850s, Woolloomooloo Bay was crammed with ships unloading merchandise and migrants from all over the world. Today, Woolloomooloo is in the midst of a complete about-face. From tough commercial district to select residential area, the old 'Loo is changing and — not before time either. Throughout the 1930s, the name Woolloomooloo was synonymous with thugs and criminals. Today, it is almost genteel, with new public housing sympathetically designed to blend in with the Victorian terraces that give the old waterfront neighbourhood its distinctive character.

A lightly-laden freighter noses warily up the long ellipse of Woolloomooloo Bay, past the Naval Dockyard at Garden Island and the green peninsula that marks the eastern boundary of The Domain.

(Left) Mooching home under a big blue kite emblazoned with the stars of the Southern Cross, a racer heads for the Cruising Yacht Club in Rushcutters Bay.

The

Eastern Shore

Majestic Macquarie Light, one of the biggest and most beautiful on the coast, was commissioned in 1883 on the site of Australia's first lighthouse, designed by the emancipated convict architect, Francis Greenway.

(Overleaf) At dusk, the view from the front porch of Doyle's restaurant at Watson's Bay induces a heady feeling of distance as diners contemplate the water views.

circumstance of looking for a sail would bring one into view.'' But Hunter's flagstaff was found to be too short to be properly seen by incoming ships and in September that year, Phillip went down to South Head to select a more suitable spot on which to erect a brick column 10 metres high.

Whenever I see the signal flags stretched out in the wind, my mind goes to the homesick longing in that vivid entry in Watkin Tench's journal: ''Here on the summit of the hill, every morning from daylight till the sun sunk, did we sweep the horizon in hope of seeing a sail. At every fleeting speck which arose from the bosom of the sea, the heart bounded and the telescope was lifted to the eye. If a ship appeared here, we knew she must be bound to us . . .''

At last, on June 3 1790 the shout of ''The flag's up!'' resounded through the settlement. Tench scrambled up to the heights above Dawes Point and through his glass, saw the flag at South Head. ''A brother officer was with me,'' he wrote. ''We could not speak; we wrung each other by the hand with hearts and eyes overflowing.'' As it turned out the incoming ships of the Second Fleet brought not much more than death and disease. Certainly there were precious few provisions. But at least there were letters from home.

Tench tells us that ''Letters! Letters!'' was the cry. ''They were produced and torn open in trembling agitation,'' he says. ''News burst upon us like meridian splendours upon a blind man. We were overwhelmed with it, public, private, general and particular. Not . . . until some days had elapsed were we able to methodise it or reduce it into form.''

Major-General Lachlan Macquarie — ''Macquarie the Builder'' — was NSW Governor for 12 years from 1810 to 1821. He had an immediate and lasting impact on South Head generally and Watson's Bay in particular. The first road built to his order was Old South Head Road, 13 kilometres of twists and turns that follow the hilltops and ridges from Hyde Park to the hill above Watson's Bay. One of the more remarkable facts about Old South Head Road, apart from the unrivalled views it commands as it snakes upward between Double Bay and Rose Bay, is that it was constructed in just 10 weeks, not by gangs of convicts but by 25 soldiers from Macquarie's own 73rd Regiment, the Highlanders. The road enabled official and commercial communication to pass quickly between Sydney and Watson's Bay where incoming ships often anchored for days to await clearance or a favourable breeze to take them on up the harbour to Sydney Cove.

Not far from the signal station at Outer South Head stands Macquarie Light, surely one of the world's most noble lighthouses. It was designed by the father of Australian architecture, the convicted forger Francis Greenway, whose memory lives in many of Sydney's most beautiful Georgian buildings. Construction was completed in just 17 months and the lighthouse, known then simply as Macquarie Tower, was officially opened on December 16 1817 when Governor Macquarie, his wife and an official party left Sydney Cove at dawn and made their way by horse and carriage along Old South Head Road to Watson's Bay. Macquarie ''delivered Mr Greenway his emancipation this day'', then sat down with the newly-freed man to breakfast with him.

The harbour is cleaner now than at any time since the start of European settlement.

The oil light and lens were installed in 1818 and maintained by dues of twopence a ton being levied on the gross tonnage of all incoming vessels. The first lighthouse keeper was Robert Watson, for whom the lovely bay beneath the light is

named. Watson, who had arrived in the colony 30 years before as a quartermaster aboard HMS *Sirius* and had served as a pilot and Sydney's Harbourmaster, was in the position barely 12 months before he died. Down at Watson's Bay, beneath a huge Moreton Bay fig, said to have sheltered Macquarie and his party during a picnic in 1811, is a tablet recording Watson's contribution to the district and the harbour's history.

The original whitewashed stone lighthouse stood on its two-hectare plot for 65 years. In 1883 it was demolished and another of identical design (save for a tower 26 metres high — three metres taller than the original and powered by electric light) was constructed immediately behind and close to the old building. When the Premier, Sir Henry Parkes, laid the foundation stone on March 1 1880 he quoted Longfellow's poem, The Lighthouse:

> "Steadfast, serene, immovable, the same
> Year after year, through all the silent night,
> Burns on for evermore that quenchless flame,
> Shines on that inextinguishable light."

The present light throws its 1 140 000 candlepower beam more than 45 kilometres out to sea in clear weather. Revolving slowly, it gives those out to sea a distinctive wink, flashing twice every 10 seconds.

Watson's Bay is also the home of the harbour's pilot boats, the plucky little vessels that put to sea no matter what the weather to guide ships safely into the port. As a young journalist way back in the days when many people preferred to travel by ship and not plane, I was often sent down the harbour by Stannard's launch to cover their arrival. From the launch, hove-to in the relative calm between the Heads, I marvelled at the courage of the pilots who had no hesitation in going straight out to sea, no matter what the weather, to meet the ships in the offing. Once they were alongside, rising and plunging against the sheer steel wall of the ship's topsides, they leapt from the pilot boat and clung like monkeys to the swaying Jacob's Ladder as they scrambled up into the waiting arms of the crew. There were occasions, especially when the big white Matson liners, the *Mariposa* and the *Monterey*, arrived with their American celebrities aboard, that I had to follow the pilot's example and jump for dear life to get aboard, conduct my interviews, scribble my story and be able to file it by telephone by the time the ship berthed at Woolloomooloo.

Harbour pilotage seems to have been a matter of catch-as-catch-can — until 1834 when a public outcry over the wreck of the full-rigged ship *Edward Lombe* forced the government to roster pilots around the clock. Two other disasters within two months of each other in 1857 — the loss of 121 lives aboard the British emigrant ship, *Dunbar*, at The Gap, and the loss of 21 lives when the Aberdeen clipper, *Catherine Adamson*, went aground on Middle Head, forced further improvements to the pilot service including the establishment of vital navigation lights within the harbour.

One of the immediate consequences of the *Edward Lombe* disaster was the stationing of a lightship, the old schooner, *Rose*, off the Sow and Pigs, the shoal and rocks just inside South Head which divides

Hornby Light, literally the most colourful of all Sydney's lighthouses. Built in 1858 as a sequel to the tragic losses of two vessels, it lights inner South Head and South Reef.

(Left) The most popular seafood restaurant in Sydney, Doyle's On The Beach at Watson's Bay, boasts a location probably unrivalled anywhere else in Australia.

the harbour fairway into two channels. The *Rose* remained on-station at the reef for 20 years until her flashing red light was replaced in 1856 by the hulk of the former survey cutter, HMS *Bramble*. Her lights shone their warning on the reef for 21 years before she was replaced with another lightship of the same name which was to serve for an extraordinary 35 years until she too was replaced in 1912 by the no doubt more efficient but decidedly less romantic acetylene gas-powered light buoys.

No vessel can truly be said to have entered Sydney Harbour until the picturesque red and white vertically striped Hornby Light is on her port beam. The light is named for Lady Denison, the wife of the Governor and daughter of Admiral Sir Phipps Hornby, who in the 1860s commanded the Royal Navy's Sydney-based Pacific Fleet. It is perhaps the harbour's most distinctive light and was one of those erected in 1858 following the wrecks of the *Dunbar* and the *Catherine Adamson*. Its primary purpose is to mark the southern headland but it also serves to light the treacherous South Reef which stretches its tentacles of oyster-covered rocks more than 30 metres from the shore. Although Hornby Light's warning of danger could scarcely be more obvious, the reef continues to be a place where experienced yachtsmen and amateurs alike pile up in attempts to cut corners in ocean races.

South of Watson's Bay, past Village Point, is the long inlet known as Parsley Bay, named by Phillip's boatcrew who explored it on January 22 1788. Convicts sent down to the fishing grounds at South Head harvested the wild parsley which grew in abundance along the shores of the narrow, steep-sided inlet. Today Parsley Bay is one of the most popular harbourside picnic areas in Sydney's Eastern Suburbs.

Not far from Parsley Bay is Vaucluse, now the site of some of Australia's richest real estate but also a place steeped in history. I somehow fancy the ghost of Sir Henry Brown Hayes, the old Irish rogue who named the place, is still there and causing all manner of Gaelic mischief. Hayes is the central character in what might be called a classic Irish story, as fantastic as it is true. In 1797, 35-year-old Hayes, who had been Sheriff of the ancient city of Cork and Captain of the Militia, became a widower. He was a man of considerable passion and despite his bereavement, or perhaps because of it, he immediately fell in love with a Miss Mary Pike, an heiress who happened to be visiting mutual friends in Cork.

Impatient with the time-consuming rituals of 18th century wooing, Hayes had Pike kidnapped and brought to his estate where a man dressed as a priest attempted to carry out a "marriage" service. The unwilling bride was rescued the next day and Hayes fled. A reward of £1000 was offered for his apprehension. Three years later, Hayes walked into a hairdressing salon in Cork and gave himself up to the barber who, at Hayes's suggestion, turned him in and subsequently collected the reward — a fortune which enabled the lucky barber to build three handsome Georgian cottages which still stand in Cork's Grand Parade. Hayes was found guilty and condemned to death, a sentence which was commuted to transportation for life. He arrived in Sydney in July 1802 aboard the convict ship, *Atlas*.

Thirteen months later he bought at auction two farms near Parsley Bay and joined them into a single 190-hectare estate crowned by a splendid Georgian house to which he gave the name Vaucluse. Why Vaucluse? According to Vince Kelly's excellent *History of Woollahra* there are two suggestions, both associated with the Italian lyric poet and scholar Petrarch. One is that Hayes took the name from Vaucluse, a town in France to which the poet retreated in 1337. Vaucluse is derived from the Latin, *vallis clausa*, meaning a closed valley. It is claimed by some that Hayes visited the place after he fled from Ireland. The other suggestion is that the name derives from Petrarch's sonnet, The Hermit of Vaucluse.

(Right) When the pioneer solo circumnavigator, Joshua Slocum, sailed into Sydney Harbour in the 1890s he marvelled that every man and boy either had a boat of their own or sailed with a friend. Nothing has changed.

(Overleaf) From Tivoli Avenue, Vaucluse, the view across Rose Bay embraces racing yachts locked in waterborne combat. The racing, conducted on the harbour year-round, involves boats of all shapes and sizes.

GEORGETTE

Perched high on a green ridge beyond New South Head Road, the magnificent Rose Bay convent stands like a Scottish castle lording it over a silver loch.

(Overleaf) Mid-week twilight racing on the harbour has proved a spectacular success. Here, yachts from the Sydney Amateur Sailing Club, one of the oldest on the harbour, beat up toward a mark in Rose Bay.

I put my money on the second explanation. Hayes's antics in Sydney give every indication that quite apart from his Irishness, the man was suffering from what used to be called dementia. Governor King is therefore believed to have allowed him to take up the land at the far end of the harbour as a convenient method of banishment for the "gentleman convict". Hayes continued to make a nuisance of himself, persisting, against the Governor's orders, in what was the first attempt to found a Masonic lodge in Australia. During the clash between Governor William Bligh and the rebellious officers of the NSW Corps in 1808, Hayes supported Bligh and was consequently banished to Newcastle.

Under Governor Macquarie, Hayes was permitted to return to his farm but there he found the estate overrun with "swarms of enormous serpents". He complained of waking up to find "a gentleman six feet long and as black as coal, coiled up on my white counterpane and another of the same dimensions underneath the bed".

His solution was an obvious one for any Irishman with a belief in the mystical powers of St Patrick. With Governor Macquarie's bemused indulgence, Hayes imported 500 tonnes of genuine Irish bog. The soil, in biscuit barrels, was taken down to Vaucluse by boat and placed in a trench dug around the house. Hayes superintended the work and kept a crowd of spectators amused with running commentaries and songs about the saint and his wonderful powers in having driven the snakes from Ireland. Hayes was eventually pardoned and 12 years later when he had returned to Ireland and the estate was taken over by Customs Collector Captain John Piper, Piper could report, in all seriousness, that Vaucluse was no longer infested with vipers.

In 1827, the house at Vaucluse and 40 hectares surrounding it were bought by William Charles Wentworth, the Australian-born explorer, poet, barrister and fiery advocate of Australian political independence, who within two years built Vaucluse House, the fine colonial mansion which today is open to the public.

Nielsen Park stretches all the way from the Bottle and Glass Rocks (named by watermen because of their fanciful shape) on Vaucluse Point, through Shark Bay and Steel Point to the Hermitage Foreshore Reserve in Hermit Bay. It is a supremely beautiful place combining well-kept lawns and native trees with access to the gloriously golden Shark Beach, safely netted for year-round swimming. We owe its existence to the far-sighted Neil Rasmus Wilson Nielsen, the former union organiser who became Minister of Lands in the McGowan Labor Government of 1910–11. Nielsen, one of the first to use the term "national park", was a passionate advocate of harbourside reservations. He authorised the creation of the park that now bears his name through the acquisition of private properties, including those of the badly-neglected Wentworth estate, along the foreshore. Although there are plenty of references to sharks here (Shark Point, Shark Beach and just out in the harbour's eastern channel, Shark Island) the names do not indicate that sharks are more plentiful here than they are anywhere else. In fact no shark attacks have been recorded.

Beyond Hermit Point lies the great arc of Rose Bay. The harbour's biggest bay, its perfect crescent boasts an excellent beach that stretches for more than two kilometres. The name Rose Bay was in use as early as 1796 and is believed to have been bestowed by Governor Phillip in honour of George (later Sir George) Rose who was Under-Secretary for the Treasury when the First Fleet was being outfitted. Phillip also honoured Rose by naming the Parramatta settlement, Rose Hill, after him.

Rose Bay's Aboriginal name was the much more interesting *"Pan-ner-rong"*, which meant blood. According to Vince Kelly's *History of Woollahra*, this was the site often chosen by the Aboriginals as a battle ground or for ritualised inter-tribal fighting. According to Keith Willey, payback feuds might extend through generations but Aboriginal wars were seldom very bloody. "Because of the constant struggle for existence, no tribe could afford to lose too may hunters," he says. "Spears would be thrown — and dodged, or deflected

Point Piper's luxurious apartments bask in the sunshine high above Double Bay. Double Bay is, as its name suggests, two bays in one and one of the biggest and most capacious in the harbour.

by shields. Sometimes the warriors would close in, swinging their long-handled clubs. One or a few men might die, then one side or the other would break and run. The victims seldom followed, for success in battle was something to be celebrated at once in corroboree, before the admiring gaze of the women.''

The first European residents in Rose Bay were the salt-boilers sent down at the turn of the 19th century to exploit the extensive salt deposits along the foreshores. The land was divided into several large grants whose imposing stone homesteads can still be seen on the high ground overlooking the harbour. Throughout the Second World War, Rose Bay's huge expanse of smooth water was constantly busy with the arrival and departure of military seaplanes, particularly the Catalinas and others taking Australian and American troops to the New Guinea campaign between 1942 and 1945. It was also the home of the enormous, lumbering Sunderlands which pioneered the commercial air routes between the UK and Sydney. The Flying Boat Base became as familiar to Sydney people as Pinchgut.

Ruth Park recalls flying in ''the old girls'' as they were affectionately known. ''The bellow of those archaic engines, the ostentatious clouds of spray, the lumbering rush across the pearly blue bay! Will she make it? Can she make it? Can she possibly? It is like watching a turtle trying to fly. And those of us who so intrepidly pioneered the flying-boat route remember the anguished clutching of the seat arm, trying to lift, lift, lift the great deadweight . . . then the falling away of the water, the clearing of sea-wet windows, aloft into the smogless yonder in a wonderful plane that seated 20 passengers, might not have been as speedy as land-based craft but was, after all, *safe*.''

Point Piper is one of Sydney's most densely populated headlands. Apartment towers and blocks of flats dominate a tiny area blessed with one of the most stunning views anywhere on the harbour. But it wasn't always so crowded. In the early years of the 19th century, the point — shaped appropriately like a bagpipe — and all the property between William Street, Double Bay, Ocean Street, Jersey Road to Oxford Street and Old South Head Road as far as Rose Bay belonged to just one man, Captain John Piper, the Collector of Customs who became known as ''the Prince of Australia''.

Piper, a Scot, who arrived in Sydney in 1791 as a poor, 18-year-old ensign, was at the age of 41 appointed Macquarie's ''Naval Officer'', a job which carried a hefty incentive. Piper was allowed a commission of five per cent on all the customs and harbour dues he collected. Within a few short years he was earning what was, for the 1840s, the staggering sum of £4000 a year. He built a magnificent house on the point that was to take his name and called it Henrietta Villa. It was surrounded by ''a most excellent garden which supplies an abundance of the choicest fruits, peaches, apricots and nectarines and every other species . . .'' The scene of dazzling entertainments, the house and its estate carried more than 100 servants and its own stable of racing thoroughbreds.

Piper's extravagance came crashing down when the martinet Governor Darling ordered an investigation of Piper's accounts. Although no dishonesty was uncovered, some carelessness and neglect gave Darling all the excuse he needed to dismiss Piper. Financial catastrophe soon followed and Piper was forced to sell his property. Piper decided that suicide was the only way out. He had his boatmen row him out to the middle of the harbour and having commanded his piper to play a lament, threw himself overboard. The boatmen, however, could not bear to see it all end like this so they fished him out and rowed him ashore. Piper died a pauper in 1851 at the age of 78.

Henrietta Villa survived Piper by only a few years before it was torn down and replaced with an even more splendid mansion, Woollahra House, which stood alone on the point until 1929. Woollahra House's long, tree-lined drive is now the boomerang-shaped Wunulla Road. Turn into Wunulla Road off New South Head Road and there on the corner, disguised these days as the Rose Bay Police Station, is the wonderful old cottage that once served as the gatekeeper's lodge of Woollahra House.

At the very tip of Point Piper is Lady Martin's Beach, named for the widow of the 19th century Liberal MLA, Sir James Martin, who leased Woollahra House in the 1890s. Above the beach is the clubhouse of the Royal Prince Edward Yacht Club formed in 1920 and named in honour of Edward, Prince of Wales and later King Edward VIII, who visited Australia that year and agreed to become the club's patron.

Lawrence Hargrave, astronomer, engineer, explorer and Australia's great aviation pioneer, lived at 58 Wunulla Road from 1902 until his death in 1915. Hargrave was one of those noble souls who believed in sharing his scientific knowledge for the benefit of mankind and without any thoughts of money-making. When Wilbur Wright contacted him in 1900 about the use of his aircraft models, Hargrave told the American inventor he had no patents and his aeronautical discoveries were ''at the disposal of all''.

But Hargrave, variously described as ''a charming and absent-minded man'', and ''the crank with the kite'', was concerned with marine engineering as well as aviation and even went so far as to invent a pair of inflatable rubber shoes, like large tennis rackets, which enabled him to stroll about the waters of the harbour.

Although a recess on its southern shore is named Blackburn Bay after David Blackburn, Sailing Master aboard HMS *Supply* in 1788, Double Bay is not a double bay in the strictest topographical sense. The mouth of the bay, between Point Piper and Darling Point, is less than a kilometre wide but the bay has a delightful shoreline that curves around in a great arc for the best part of three kilometres. On its eastern shore lies the narrow, sandy crescent known as Seven Shillings Beach. In her book, *Point Piper, Past and Present*, Nesta Griffiths explains that the Busby family, who owned the Redleaf estate, paid the traditional Aboriginal owner, a man known to them only as Gurrah, the sum of seven shillings for the fishing rights to the beach.

Double Bay offers what is, without question, the best but also the most expensive shopping in Sydney. Its shops and boutiques, its hairdressers and its restaurants often seem to sell things which are at least twice the price asked anywhere else. Hence its tag: Double Pay. But one of the nicest things in Double Bay is not its trendy shops and eateries; it is the extraordinary anachronism at the end of Bay Street. The NSW 18ft Sailing League's weatherboard headquarters, protruding out into the water on so many piles, is essentially a working man's club, poker machines, frothing beer and all, its smoky old bar adorned with sepia-tinted pictures of the colossal old sail-carrying eighteens. And in its tiny cafe, which serves probably the most succulent grilled jewfish cutlets in Sydney, the seafood is always superbly cooked and beautifully presented. The Eighteens is an institution which has been part of the Double Bay landscape since the 1930s, and one hopes will continue to be so. Certainly the harbour would not be quite the same without those skittish creatures whizzing down the wind under their billowing kites on weekend races. The super-flyers stage what is certainly the fastest competition on the harbour.

Seven Shillings Beach got its name, so the story goes, because of the price said to have been paid to Aboriginal inhabitants in the 1840s.

(Right) Double Bay, one of Sydney's most expensive suburbs, offers the very wealthy the ultimate in ironical status symbols, pools beside the harbour.

The Northern Beaches and

Manly

NO OTHER CITY IN THE WORLD is blessed with as many glorious golden beaches as those found around Sydney's northern coastline. In the 25 kilometres from Manly to Palm Beach there are no fewer than 11 major surfing beaches and several other smaller beaches, all of them flanked by bold headlands each with its own unique features. Manly is so big it has been divided into two — South Steyne and North Steyne. This was the birthplace of surf bathing in Australia, the activity indulged in by virtually everyone, young and old alike. Surfing (not surfboard riding but plain old swimming in the surf) is not so much a sport as a national pastime, the birthright of every Aussie kid and something which is very much taken for granted. Which is why it comes as something of a shock for most people when they are told that until 1902, public swimming was formally forbidden by law. Whoever sanctioned the Act of 1838 which made it illegal for anyone to swim in public except in the hours of darkness (8pm to 6am) must (by today's standards) have had a highly developed sense of prudery. The Victorians not only thought it undignified to swim in the ocean but positively, outrageously indecent!

But then in 1902, a journalist, William Gocher, the editor of the local newspaper, *The Manly Daily*, decided it was high time that one of the most absurd aspects of Victorian morality was knocked on the head. Gocher did something that no one else had been game to do. He defied the law by plunging into the surf at Manly. Gocher no doubt knew a good story when he saw one. He frolicked in the waves for a time and then came out to sit on the sand and wait for the police. They never came. Soon, hundreds and then thousands of Sydneysiders leapt at the opportunity to enjoy what had been denied them since the earliest days of the colony — a chance to enjoy the magnificent surfing beaches.

It was the US Olympic swimming champion and native Hawaiian, Duke Kahanamoku, who introduced surfboard riding to Australians at Manly in the '20s. Manly can also claim to have been the birthplace of what has become known throughout the swimming world as the Australian crawl or freestyle. It was the New Hebridean, Tommy Tanna, who introduced it, in the 1890s at Manly Baths.

The journey north from Manly to Palm Beach is a magnificent one by sea. I have sailed up and down that stretch of coast a hundred times and on each occasion some new facet of bluff and beach reveals itself. Once past the gut-wrenching grease-slick and stench of the sewerage outlet off Blue Fish Point, the water is clean and clear and dark green. Out there, on a clear, sunny day with a cool nor'easter blowing, yachtsmen find all manner of sea birds and marine life bobbing on the surface for the sheer joy of it. I have seen great mottled grey-green whale sharks 20 metres long snoozing not far from a family of turtles so ancient they had barnacles on their shell backs. Mother Carey's Chickens, otherwise known as sooty terns, dart in and out of the wave troughs, skimming up to the foaming crest and sliding down the other side, lazily trailing a wing tip in the water as they bank and wheel, looking for fish.

The journey by road, in many places right beside the ocean, is every bit as spectacular. Ruth Park aptly likened the mighty headlands to the blunt foreheads of sperm whales, butting out into the hazy blue Pacific. "The endless miles of surf belting in on beaches white as sugar, each breaker trailing its spray like smoke, bring to the spirit a joy that is a species of mild intoxication," she says.

At the height of summer, space is at a premium on Manly Beach. Surfers and family paddlers alike acclaim Manly as one of the best, safest and most popular in Sydney.

(Pages 168–169) Dee Why Head stands guard at the northern end of Curl Curl Beach. Surely poet John Masefield had such a spot in mind when he wrote his haunting epic, *Spanish Waters.* The treasure here lies in the golden beach and emerald sea.

(Left) Narrabeen Lakes pour into the sea across a sandy bar. The outfall can be treacherous and yet it is nevertheless a favourite spot for youngsters who enjoy the rush and tumble of the simulated rapids.

BENNETT

On Narrabeen's tranquil lakes, sailors in dinghies, catamarans and all manner of small boats set out to enjoy weekends on the water. Virtually everyone, no matter what their social background or income, seems to be waterborne.

(Right) Dee Why's rocks provide ideal roosting spots for fishermen determined to hook something substantial in the open sea. Ships often stand off the coast here, waiting for berths in the harbour.

(Previous page) Out through the boiling surf at Queenscliff, three bold board riders wait patiently and not a little precariously for the ultimate wave.

Tiny Queenscliff Bay gives way to Curl Curl Beach, and north again around Dee Why Head there lies the far expanse of golden sand that is partly Dee Why Beach and partly Long Reef. Behind the beach lies Dee Why Lagoon, once the nesting place for majestic black swans, ibis and ducks of all descriptions. There are those who believe that it was this lagoon, and not Narrabeen, that Governor Phillip saw on the overland trek in which he failed to reach Pittwater from Manly. No one knows how Dee Why got its name, but the most plausible of the many explanations is that it is an anglicised corruption of the Aboriginal word "Diwai", which referred to the saltwater grebes which flocked there in their thousands during the first half of the 19th century.

Around treacherous Long Reef Point is Collaroy Beach, the spot where the steamer *Collaroy* was swept ashore in 1882. Two years later she was refloated, refitted and once again set to work tramping the world's oceans. She eventually went down off California's Humboldt Reef, although one of her great iron anchors, taken ashore when she was beached here, still adorns the yard of Narrabeen Public School.

Narrabeen Lakes, a vast saltwater expanse still rimmed by beautiful bushland and which Phillip in 1788 compared to the Italian lakes, lie directly behind the beach of the same name that takes over from Collaroy and stretches all the way north to Narrabeen Head. Narrabeen is named for an Aboriginal woman who in 1818 warned European settlers of the presence there of runaway convicts.

Above Narrabeen lies Mona Vale, then Bungan Beach, Bungan Head, Newport Beach, Bilgola, Avalon, Careel Head, Whale Beach and finally glorious Palm Beach and the reassuring bulk of Barrenjoey with its towering stone lighthouse, completed in 1881 and standing 113 metres above sea level. All these beaches and indeed all the land between Narrabeen and McCarr's Creek on Pittwater was promised by Governor Macquarie to Father J. J. Therry (pronounced Terry), an Irishman and the first "official" Catholic priest in Australia. Macquarie's successor, Governor Richard Bourke, honoured the promise and in 1856 the sale of some of this land provided the funds to build Sydney's splendid Romanesque cathedral, St Mary's, just off the south end of Macquarie Street.

Surveyor Govett, who came up the peninsula in 1829, described the precipitous countryside: ". . . masses of rock in some instances appear like the castellated ruins of a fortress with dilapidated walls and shattered battlements — perpendicular in some places, sloping in others — and receding into caves overhung by huge and massive canopies which may almost be taken for the workmanship of man. These caves or hollows are called by the natives gibbie gunyahs or homes of rock, under which they occasionally put in a night."

There is precious little of that kind of countryside left on the peninsula and today, particularly around exclusive Palm Beach, the modern gibbie gunyahs tend to be valuable real estate in the shape of million-dollar homes.

Behind Palm Beach and stretching south and west in an infinity of heavily-wooded bays and coves, lies Pittwater, Broken Bay and the magnificent natural beauty of the Ku-Ring-Gai National Park.This is the way Sydney Harbour must have looked before European development. Through the broad expanse of Broken Bay and off to the west lies the wide mouth of the Hawkesbury River, while just to the south and parallel with Pittwater proper, the sinews of Cowan Creek stretch all the way back to Bobbin Head.

There, in the creek's headwaters, the Halvorsens, one of the best-known names in Australian wooden boat building, have established a base for their armada of hire boats that can be chartered to chug up and down the secluded waterway in a marvellous escape from big city pressures.

(Above left) Hidden deep within the magnificent bushland of the Ku-ring-gai Chase National Park, Coal and Candle Creek is one of the most popular anchorages for Sydney's cruising yachtsmen.

(Left) Bush-covered Barrenjoey Head blocks the sea breeze and throws a cloak of calm over Pittwater which, fringed by Ku-ring-gai Chase National Park, remains one of the best and safest cruising grounds in Australia.

(Left) Lion Island, forever crouching like its namesake, stands guard at the entrance to Pittwater and the Hawkesbury River. The island is inhabited only by nesting seabirds.

Manly made its way into the European history of Australia even before Sydney did. Phillip and the men in that first exploring party he commanded north from Botany Bay, landed at what is generally believed to have been Little Manly Cove, on January 21 1788. Ruth Park takes us back: "One can imagine that summer day, with an opaline haze of heat over the far ridges, and the three little boats beetling past the towering wall of North Head — Boree, the Enduring, the elder Australians had named it — to come at last to a delicious stillness of deep bays and bosky inlets. No doubt the magpies were clanging, the dark bush snowed-over here and there with apple gum bloom, and the grass trees marching down the slopes like a troop of kobolds."

There, either in Manly Cove or in Little Manly Cove, just to the east, Phillip had his first close encounter with the Sydney Harbour Aboriginals. He was deeply impressed by the "confidence and manly behaviour" of about 20 men who left their weapons on the beach and, stark naked save for their ornaments, fearlessly waded out in the cool, clear water to meet him. Phillip recorded that "the same people afterwards joined us when we dined" and that because of their "lively curiosity" he had to draw a circle in the sand and indicate to them that they had to stay outside it. Phillip and his men camped there that night.

Phillip was to return to Manly several times — once with nearly fatal consequences. On April 15 1788 he led a party exploring an overland route from Manly to Pittwater. The party did not reach Pittwater but Phillip did at least have the satisfaction of discovering Narrabeen's magnificent saltwater lake, which was teeming with wildfowl. From the coast, the party made its way to the upper reaches of Middle Harbour and then went far enough west to see the Blue Mountains before they returned to the waiting boats.

In his excellent book, *Arthur Phillip, His Voyaging*, Alan Frost recounts the almost tragic events of September 7 1790 when Phillip returned to Manly following reports that the runaways, Bennelong and Colbee, were among a large group of Aboriginals there, feasting on the carcase of a whale believed to have been washed up at what is now called Collins Beach, at the head of Spring Cove. "In an awkward encounter," Frost writes, "one Aboriginal speared him in the right shoulder. Amid an exchange of musket fire and spears, Phillip made for the boat but was hindered by the three-metre long spear striking the ground as he went. A desperate [Henry] Waterhouse (a young midshipman from the *Sirius*, succeeded in breaking the shaft and the Europeans headed for Sydney [Cove]."

Anyone who knows what a desperately long row it is between Manly and Sydney Cove will have some inkling of the frenzy with which the men must have pulled over those 12 kilometres. Phillip was bleeding profusely. So much so that as the men bent to the oars he swore a rough will. It was Surgeon William Balmain who tended Phillip when he eventually reached the settlement and discovered the wound to be not so serious as Phillip had imagined. The Governor recovered quickly and soon dismissed the idea of revenge. Instead, he set about renewing his friendly contacts with the Aboriginals. When Phillip left Sydney for London in December 1792 he took with him Bennelong and another man named Yemmerrawannie, whom Collins characterised as "much attached to his person". They went "voluntarily and cheerfully" and "withstood at the moment of their departure, the united distress of their wives, and the dismal lamentations of their friends".

Like a medieval castle, the sandstone ramparts of St Patrick's Theological College loom over the less than picturesque apartments that line Manly foreshores.

An arc of golden sand fringing crystal clear shallows. Not the Bahamas, but Shelly Beach.

(Overleaf) Backbreaking effort goes into pulling a surfboat out through breaking seas at North Steyne. The surfboats, once an integral part of most surf rescues, have been supplanted by inflatable runabouts.

Spring Cove sits just south-east of Little Manly Cove. At its southernmost limits and set amid hectares of virgin bush in the Sydney Harbour National Park, is Store Beach, one of the favourite haunts of Sydney's cruising yachtsmen and women. Store Beach is beautiful, but still further out and tucked in behind the lee of rocky Cannae Point lies Quarantine Beach, to me the most perfect spot in all the harbour. Quarantine is the kind of place in which, with just a little imagination, one might listen to the throbbing of cicadas and look out across that crystal water to the great pink angophoras rooted right in the saltwater's edge and allow oneself to fly back to a less complicated time.

Many years ago, I shared the pleasure with Ruth Park of coming ashore here. We sat high up on the beach under some ancient gums whose roots clung like iron talons to the red sandstone rocks. I have savoured that memory down the years, not because of what was said, but more because of what was left unsaid. The bush, the harbour, the sharp, tangy taste of the two in tandem, silenced us both and as I recall, left an indelible impression, as if we were in the presence of some ancient spirit, some timeless, unfathomable, ethereal quality that bound the earth and the water and the sky together as in a dream.

The Southern Beaches and

Bondi

BONDI! AROUND THE WORLD, IS there any other beach half so well known? I doubt it. Copacabana? A slum by comparison. Cannes? Not even in the same class. Costa Smeralda? Well, there is no surf for a start. No, Bondi is . . . Bondi! Not long after dawn the famous thousand metres of golden sand lies glorious in the early morning sun. Out there, beyond the first line of breakers, a gaggle of board riders loll on their bellies watching and waiting for the listless swell to erupt into something more substantial, a wave that might stir them into the paddle, crouch, stand, stoop and crash that seem to go on and on and on like a never-ending movie. Along the beach, freshly raked and now devoid of all signs of having been slept on the night before (as it so often is by Sydney's young and dispossessed), the joggers in their ones and twos and threes are out crunching up and down the water's edge. There are men and women of all ages, in and out of the water.

Seen like this, with the sun's rays just warm, I was reminded of another great dawn ritual . . . one that takes place on the banks of the holy River Ganges. Were these pilgrims not seeking purity also? There are no temples at Bondi and yet in a very real sense that's what the beach is. As the day warms up, thousands and often tens of thousands of devotees come flocking down to the sand and the surf and the sun to pay homage to the great Aussie deity of self-indulgence. And why not? Bondi is beautiful. No, that's not quite right. Bondi Beach is wonderful. Bondi, the suburb, is something else again — a terrible terracotta landscape laid down in the '20s and '30s and not much changed since.

Not so long ago, all surf rescues were carried out by the traditional belt and reel method.

(Previous page) Surfboard riding, introduced to Sydney—and Australia—by the Hawaiian Duke Kahanamoku in the 1920s, has become the closest thing Australia has to a national sport.

(Right) Bondi. Australia's most famous beach. The name is synonymous with sand and surf and suncream and these days also, unfortunately, with pollution. The beach has become the focal point in debate over sewage.

Bondi and the adjoining municipality of Waverley take their names from the great colonial estates that once sprawled right down to the water's edge. Edward Smith Hall, who in the 1820s published a newspaper known as *The Monitor*, owned one of the estates. He named it (nobody knows why) Bundi. Bundi quickly became corrupted to Bondi, a word which has in turn passed into Australia's ocker lexicon. Today, Bondi means Beach, Birds, Booze although not necessarily in that order.

To the southward, between Bondi and Botany Bay lie some of the finest surfing beaches in the world. Their names may not have attained the legendary proportions of Bondi, but they are not far behind. Bronte, Tamarama, Coogee and Maroubra each has its army of loyal devotees, many of whom would not dare to be seen on any other beach. There are board riders at Bronte who will tell you the waves there are the finest in the world. At Maroubra, they say, body surfing is the best. The boasts may be empty and yet to the surfing aficionados, they contain essential truth.

Most people never get the chance to see the beaches from the seaward side. Out there, with the great Pacific swells butting against the unyielding sandstone cliffs and

AMPIONS 1931

bouncing back in a terrible joggle, it is not hard to see why so many sailors — even the best of them — get sick and yield their lunch to the sea. And yet off the shelving beaches there is a wonderful undulating rhythm to the waves, a regular rise and fall that is a joy to sail in. From a couple of kilometres out, Bondi and the other beaches are often veiled in a soft white gauze of salt, haze and heat.

In Bondi, I am told, windows are left perpetually locked. Not because of burglars, but something much more insidious. Salt. Salt apparently creeps in through the slightest crack, rusting television sets, false teeth and cutlery. Well, so they say.

One of the most extraordinary sights from the seaward side is the great white scar that marks Waverley Cemetery. Seen from a distance, all those marble tombstones and slabs resemble a mighty grey mudslide that seems to cascade down the steep hills into the very sea, pounding at the base of the cliffs. The cemetery, which occupies a magnificent site with views up and down the coast, has to be one of the ugliest sights in Sydney. I say *one* of the ugliest, because not far away a procession of grotesque flats and apartment blocks, great slab-faced edifices erected in the anything-goes '50s, stand as hideous monuments to rapacious developers, insensitive councils, and architects who really should have stuck to Meccano modelling.

Beyond all that, one thing stands in triumph. The sea, majestic, bottle-green and sometimes hewn from the coldest and darkest cobalt, remains the one immutable constant. Despite the horrors of the sewerage outfall system that daily pumps billions of litres of sludgy waste into it, the Pacific still manages to sparkle. That is something uniquely Sydney.

(Right, opposite) At the base of a Coogee cliff a young man lies badly injured after a fall. A paramedic administers pain-killing drugs while surf lifesavers stand by. The one way to get the injured man out is by rescue helicopter, an invaluable part of the surf lifesaving network.

(Previous page) Bondi's surf lifesavers proudly continue a tradition of voluntary public service. Although surf rescues are today most likely to be carried out with the aid of a high-powered runabout, the traditional belt and reel team remains an integral part of the formality of lifesaving carnivals.

SLSA
RESCUE
Westpac Banking

Coogee. When Arthur Streeton painted here in the 1890s, sandhills and wild scrub fringed the beach. Coogee remains one of Sydney's best and most popular beaches.

Renowned for its exhilarating waves, Bronte remains a staunch favourite among Sydney's body surfers.

(Overleaf) A glorious summer's morning on Cronulla Beach. For generations, Sydney people have taken crystal-clear water and beaches for granted. Now that environmental threats are emerging, there are growing demands that they be safeguarded.

Botany Bay

CONTAINER TERMINALS AUSTRALIA
P&O

By the time Governor Phillip and the ships of the First Fleet arrived in Botany Bay, they had voyaged more than 24 000 kilometres via Tenerife, largest of the Canary Islands, Rio de Janeiro and Cape Town, a journey that took them eight months. The 11 vessels were all at anchor in Botany Bay on January 19 1788.

Captain Cook's accounts of the bay had been, to say the very least, glowing. He had named the place Sting-Ray Harbour and reported finding "as fine a meadow as ever was seen" on its northern shore. Later, Cook amended the reference in his log and renamed it Botanist's Bay because of the "great quantity of plants which Mr (Joseph) Banks and Dr (Daniel) Solander collected in this place". However, when the official account of his voyage was ghost-written by Hawkesmore, the name was again changed to Botany Bay.

Phillip therefore had every right to feel disappointed, if not downright annoyed, when he discovered that the bay, as big as it was, was generally too shallow and much too exposed to the seas that rolled in from the east to justify it as the site upon which the colony of New South Wales was to be founded.

The official account of his voyage, published in London in 1789, stated: "The openness of this bay and the dampness of the soil, by which the people would probably be rendered unhealthy, had already determined the Governor to seek another situation. He resolved therefore to examine Port Jackson, a bay mentioned by Captain Cook as immediately to the north of this. There he hoped to find, not only a better harbour, but a fitter place for the establishment of his new government."

The rest, as they say, is history. We know what happened to Sydney but what of Botany Bay? Well, the bay is still in many respects much as Phillip found it. Plagued by pernicious currents and shifting sands, it remains a place of some danger for mariners.

The First Fleet remained at anchor there for just seven days and then was involved in an extraordinary coincidence. Not long after dawn on the 26th, at the very moment when the British ships were weighing anchors to sail up to Port Jackson, the French ships, *L'Astrolabe* and *La Boussole*, made their way into the bay. Phillip never met the French commander, the Comte de La Perouse, but the British officers did subsequently visit the Frenchmen, feasting on fish.

La Perouse spent six weeks in Botany Bay, making repairs to his ships and rebuilding the longboats damaged in a bloody clash with the natives in Samoa. They also managed to secure a rather dubious mention in Australian history when they became the first Europeans to fire on and kill Aboriginals. La Perouse's chaplain, Père Receveur, an accomplished naturalist, died in Botany Bay on February 17 1788 and was buried ashore just two weeks before the entire expedition vanished from the face of the earth on the reefs of Vanikoro in the New Hebrides, now the nation of Vanuatu.

Receveur's grave, marked by a tall stone plinth, has become something of a French national monument. Today, when-

Windsurfers enjoy a wild ride on Botany Bay. The bay that originally offered such a poor anchorage for the First Fleet is ideal for these skimmers.

(Right) The glow of dawn in the eastern sky provides an eerie backdrop for Kurnell oil refinery.

(Previous page) On a golden summer's morning with mares' tails high in a windy sky, a tug crew, snug in the relative calm of Port Botany, set about the day's business.

ever French naval vessels visit Sydney, a contingent invariably is sent to Botany Bay to mount an honour guard or at least lay a wreath and pay their respects to the first Frenchman to lose his life on Australian soil.

By far the most important of Botany's early settlers was Simeon Lord. In his *History of Botany*, Frederick Larcombe recalls that Lord, a 19-year-old sentenced to seven years' transportation over the theft of some cloth, arrived in the colony in 1791 as a servant assigned to a Captain Rowley of the New South Wales Corps. Lord survived to become "a merchant whose stores and factories were the largest in the antipodes, one whose vessels were as well known to the whales of the Antarctic and the cunning savages of New Zealand as to the 'shroffs' and 'purvoes' of Bombay".

Lord was already the wealthy emancipist when he established a fulling mill at Botany in 1815. Here, in a factory not far from the site of the present Sydney Airport, he produced "coarse cloths, blankets and flannels" dyed with extracts from Botany Bay's flora. Most of Lord's cloth went to the colonial government at two shillings and sixpence a yard plus two pounds of soap and ten pounds of copper for every 100 yards delivered. A difference with Governor Bligh over a trading matter which saw Lord spend a month in prison assured that in 1808 Lord would be a ringleader in the anti-Bligh rebellion.

The earliest development along the shores of Botany Bay included the exploitation of the extensive saltpans and of the Aboriginal shell middens used in the manufacture of lime essential to bind the mortar in the earliest buildings of the Sydney Cove settlement.

Between the 1860s and the 1890s glass, glue, soap, and tanning factories sprang up. Until comparatively recently, a journey from Botany to the Kingsford Smith International Airport, which grew out of the swampy cow pastures by the bayside, invariably involved running the gauntlet of an odoriferous two kilometres — and made the departing passengers very glad indeed to be leaving.

In 1880 a jetty known locally as Long Pier was built in what is now the suburb of Banksmeadow to handle cargoes of coal from Newcastle. At its peak the coal trade amounted to about 15 000 tonnes a year, but the coal traffic declined and eventually disappeared and the jetty has long since ceased to exist.

The Australian oil company, H. C. Sleigh, established a terminal on the banks of the Alexandria Canal in 1930, at a time when ships offloaded their refined petroleum through lighters on the bay. In 1948 BORAL set up its refinery at Matraville and seven years later at Kurnell. Today, its great orange plume of fire can be seen far out to sea.

Port Botany has assumed virtually all the burdens of Australia's major seaport formerly shouldered by Sydney Harbour. The wharf complex, with its huge gantry cranes, is spread over 260 hectares to a large extent reclaimed from the bay. West of Port Botany, the broad promenade at Brighton-Le-Sands gives way to the southern suburbs of Ramsgate, Dolls Point and Sandringham. Across the Taren Point Bridge lies Caringbah, the George's River and Port Hacking's glorious bushland fringing the southern shore of the Royal National Park.

Through all this Sydney emerges as not simply *the* most beautiful harbour in the world, but with Pittwater to the north and Botany Bay–Port Hacking to the south, three in a row. Unbeatable on their own — combined they form a unique combination which is unequalled.

Notwithstanding the giant jet aircraft that swoop low over the water, Botany Bay still tempts anglers, both amateur and professional, to cast a line.

On Pork Hacking's Gunnamatta Bay, dinghies are carefully moored to await their owners' pleasures.

(Pages 200–201) A solitary eucalypt stands like a lonely sentinel at Sutherland Point, the inner south point of Botany Bay named by Cook for a young seaman who died here aboard the *Endeavour* in 1770.

(Overleaf) At Port Botany, Australia's biggest port, a jumbo jet descends to Sydney's Kingsford Smith Airport while Japanese vessels discharge containerised cargoes.

CONTAINER TERMINALS
CONTAINE
BUNGA ANGSANA
PENANG

AUSTRALIA LIMITED
TERMINALS AUSTRALIA LIMITED
FLYING TIGERS

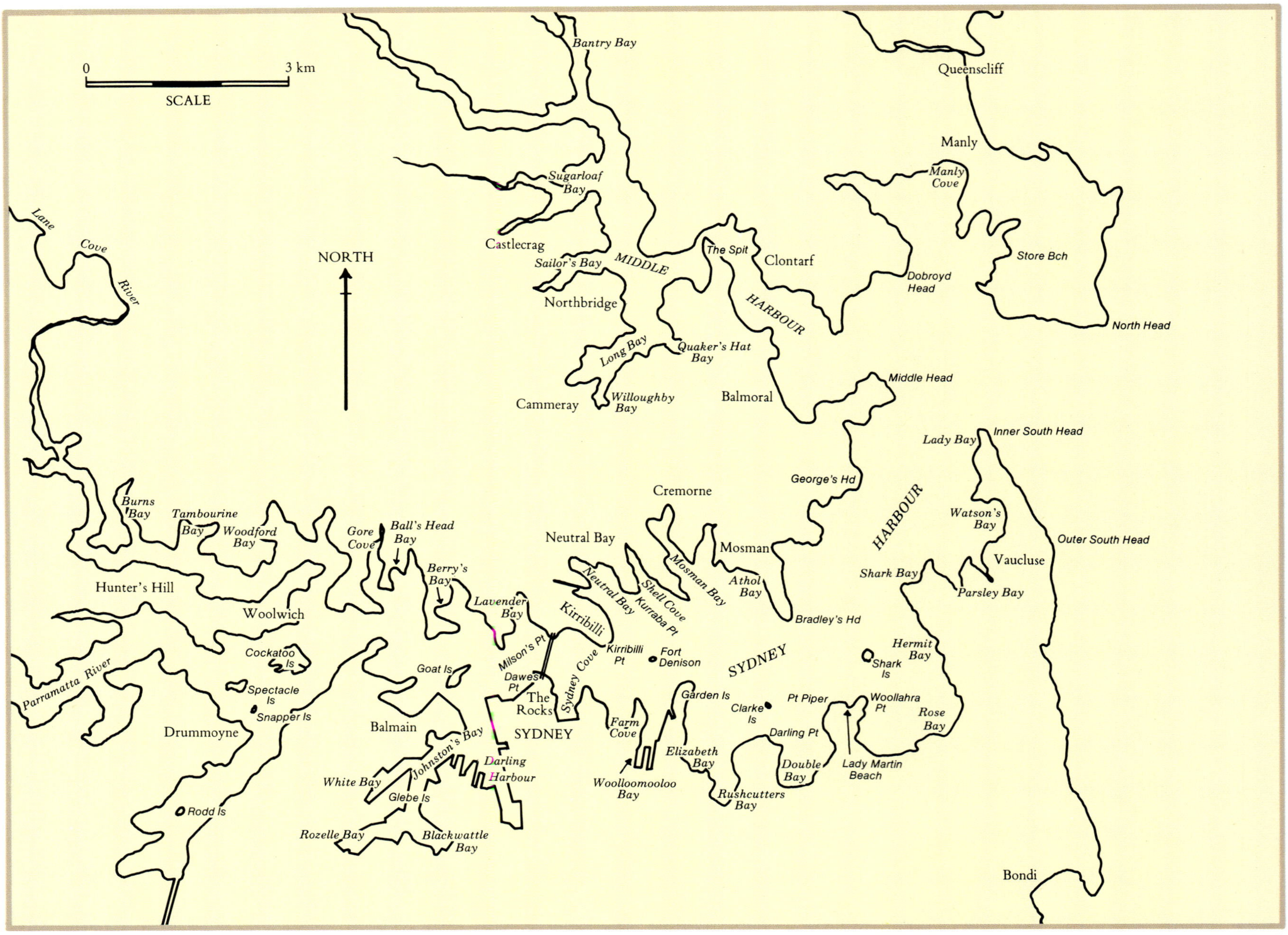

0
3 km
SCALE
NORTH
Bantry Bay
Queenscliff
Manly
Manly Cove
Sugarloaf Bay
Castlecrag
Sailor's Bay
MIDDLE
HARBOUR
The Spit
Clontarf
Dobroyd Head
Store Bch
North Head
Northbridge
Long Bay
Quaker's Hat Bay
Willoughby Bay
Cammeray
Balmoral
Middle Head
Lane Cove River
Lady Bay
Inner South Head
George's Hd
Cremorne
HARBOUR
Watson's Bay
Outer South Head
Vaucluse
Parsley Bay
Shark Bay
Burns Bay
Tambourine Bay
Woodford Bay
Gore Cove
Ball's Head Bay
Neutral Bay
Mosman
Hunter's Hill
Berry's Bay
Lavender Bay
Neutral Bay
Kurraba Pt
Shell Cove
Mosman Bay
Athol Bay
Bradley's Hd
Woolwich
Kirribilli
Milson's Pt
Kirribilli Pt
Fort Denison
SYDNEY
Hermit Bay
Shark Is
Cockatoo Is
Parramatta River
Spectacle Is
Snapper Is
Goat Is
Dawes Pt
The Rocks
Sydney Cove
Farm Cove
Garden Is
Clarke Is
Pt Piper
Woollahra Pt
Rose Bay
Drummoyne
Balmain
Johnston's Bay
SYDNEY
Darling Pt
Elizabeth Bay
Double Bay
Lady Martin Beach
White Bay
Darling Harbour
Woolloomooloo Bay
Rushcutters Bay
Glebe Is
Rodd Is
Rozelle Bay
Blackwattle Bay
Bondi

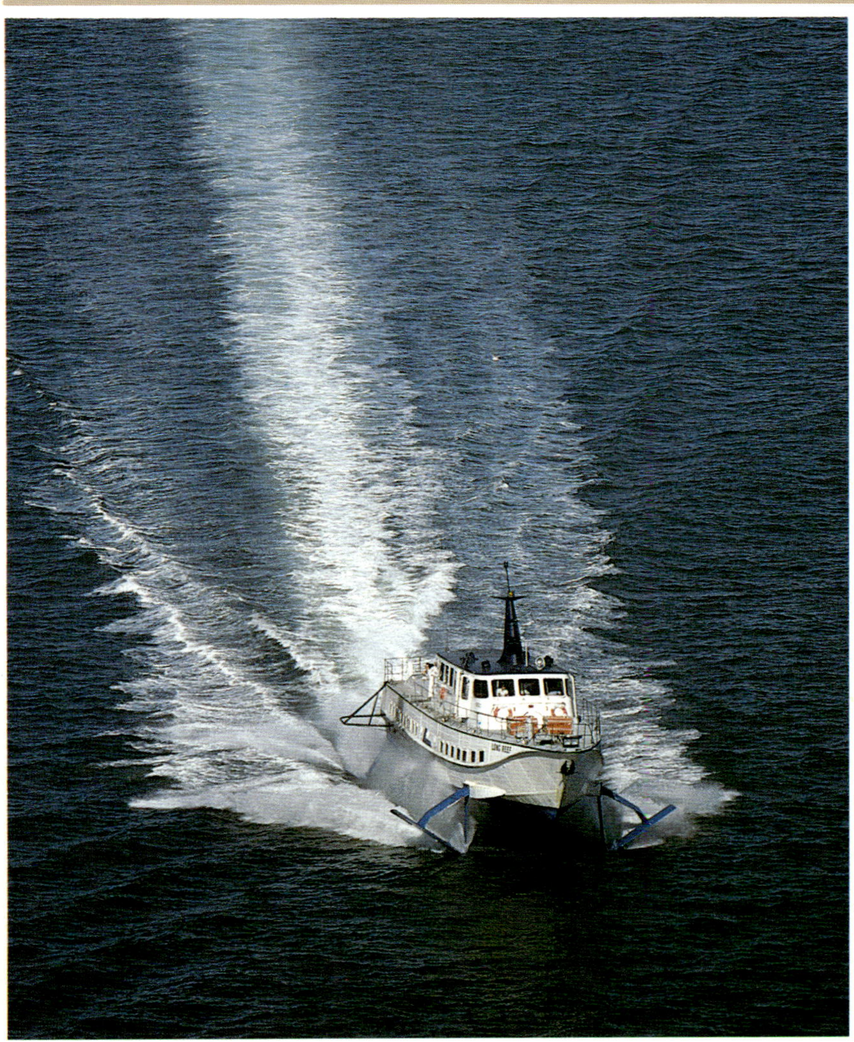

A ferry that literally flies. Riding high out of the water, hydrofoils have been skimming over the seven nautical miles between Circular Quay and Manly for more than 20 years.

Broken Bay
Berowra Ck
Cowan Ck
Palm Beach
Whale Beach
KU-RING-GAI CHASE
NATIONAL PARK
Berowra Waters
Pittwater
Avalon
Newport
Mona Vale
Bobbin Head
Narrabeen
NORTH
Collaroy
Long Reef
Dee Why
Curl Curl
Queenscliff
Manly
North Head
Sydney Harbour
South Head
Parramatta River
SYDNEY
Bondi
Tamarama
Coogee
Cook's River
Maroubra
Port Botany
Botany Bay
La Perouse
Cape Banks
Kurnell
Kurnell Peninsula
George's River
0
5 km
SCALE

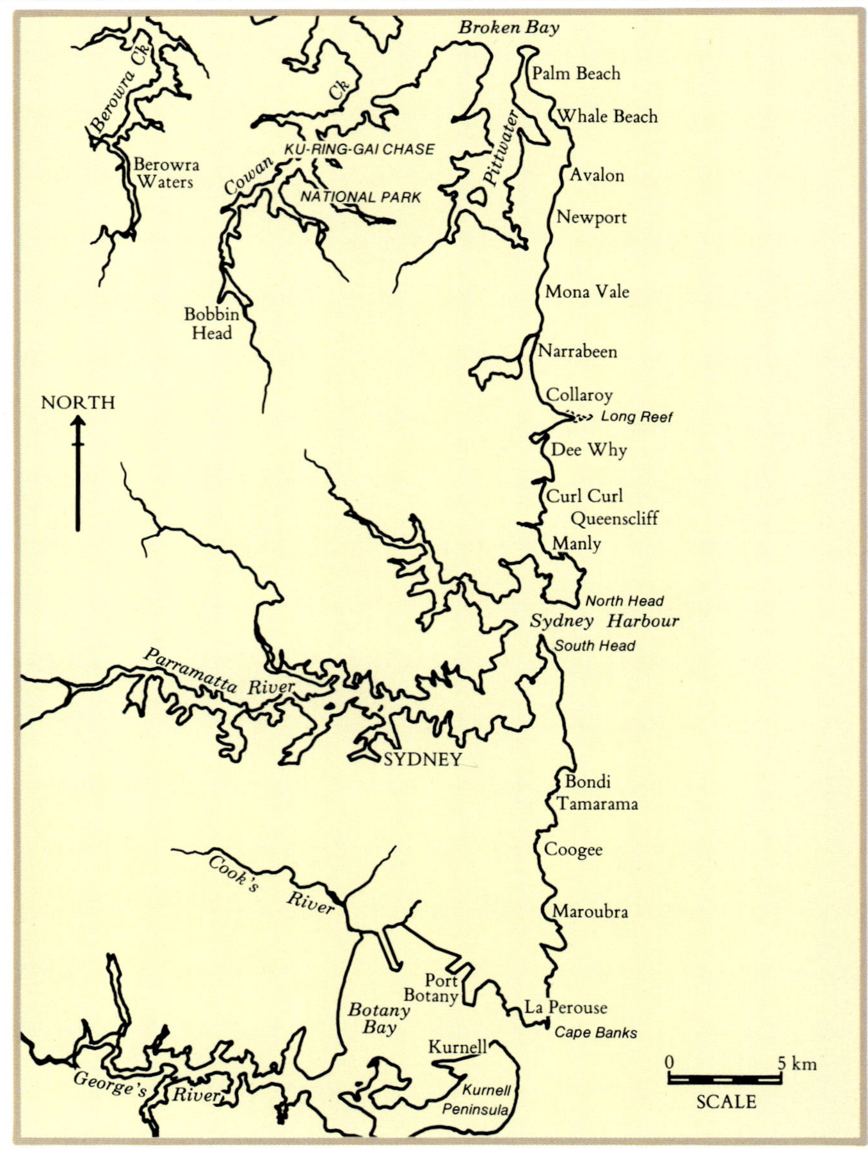

Index

INDEX

ACKNOWLEDGMENTS

Passages from *The Fatal Shore*, by Robert Hughes, are reproduced by kind permission of publishers Collins Harvill.
The author is specially indebted to Ruth Park, P. R. "Inky" Stephenson and Robert Hughes for permission to quote material from their books, *A Companion Guide to Sydney*, *A History of Sydney Harbour* and *The Fatal Shore*. Special thanks also to the Maritime Services Board of NSW for its generosity in assisting Leo Meier to capture the harbour's many moods.

Photograph Acknowledgments

Pages 54–55: Grenville Turner, Wildlight Photo Agency. Pages 65, 128, 142–3, 157: Peter Solness, Wildlight Photo Agency. Pages 82–3, 188–9: Oliver Strewe, Wildlight Photo Agency.
Pages 46–7, 60–1, 68–9, 136–7: Weldon Trannies.